EARLY YEARS
DAILY DIARY

I wish to acknowledge my gratitude to my cherished sister, illustrator and graphic designer Kim Aaronricks and my wonderful friends the Cheeky Monkeys Childminding Group for their continued support.

EARLY YEARS DAILY DIARY

KAY FISHER, EYP

authorHOUSE®

AuthorHouse™
1663 Liberty Drive
Bloomington, IN 47403
www.authorhouse.com
Phone: 1-800-839-8640

First published by AuthorHouse   10/12/2011

ISBN: 978-1-4389-4160-8 (sc)

Printed in the United States of America

Images and graphic designs © Kim Aaronricks 2011

This book is printed on acid-free paper.

Dear Parents,

An important part of your child's care involves working in partnership. This book is designed to keep you informed of your child's daily activities, achievements, experiences and other important information that you need to know about their day.

It is also designed for you to contribute to your child's experiences. If there are any particular milestones your child reaches, anything in particular you would like them to learn, or any experiences you would like to mention, please feel free to write or make notes on any of the pages in this book.

In conjunction with this, I feel it is important for you to be able to tell me anything I need to know about your child in order for me to care for them effectively, so there is also space for you to record information. Things you may like to consider are: changes in usual sleep patterns, disruptions in the child's life, if you need different drop off/pick up times for a certain day, changes in contact numbers, changes in who will pick your child up, and so on.

I hope that by using this book together, we will provide your child with a continuity of care and produce a personal record of their daily achievements, activities and development.

Please do not hesitate to talk to me about any issues or concerns you may have throughout your child's time with me.

Child's Details

Name	
Date of birth	
Address	
Contact telephone numbers	
Emergency contact password & phone numbers	
Other settings attending -Sessions & times	
Contracted childminding hours	
Additional notes; Allergies, medication details	

This weekend I...

Weekly Planning

	Trips	Activities	Notes
Monday			
Tuesday			
Wednesday			
Thursday			
Friday			

Parent's Notes

Monday

Tuesday

Wednesday

Thursday

Friday

Date [   ]

Today I have been...

Happy ☐	Chatty ☐	Quiet ☐	Sad ☐	Funny ☐	Tired ☐
Grumpy ☐	Noisy ☐	Friendly ☐	Ill ☐	Rebellious ☐	Energetic ☐

The activities I did today were...

[   ]

Today I learnt about...

[   ]

Today I have eaten...

Meal	What it was	All/most/some/none
Breakfast		
Snack		
Lunch		
Dessert		
Snack		
Dinner		
Dessert		

Please sign the medicine book ☐   Please provide some more:

Please sign the accident book ☐   _____

Today I slept...

Fell Asleep	Woke Up

Today my nappies were...

Time	Wet	Soiled	Dry	Checked

I had the following milk today...

Time	fl oz	Time	fl oz

Today I...

Went on the potty ☐   Went on the toilet ☐   I tried! ☐

Additional Notes...

Date _____

Today I have been...

Happy ☐	Chatty ☐	Quiet ☐	Sad ☐	Funny ☐	Tired ☐
Grumpy ☐	Noisy ☐	Friendly ☐	Ill ☐	Rebellious ☐	Energetic ☐

The activities I did today were...

Today I learnt about...

Today I have eaten...

Meal	What it was	All/most/some/none
Breakfast		
Snack		
Lunch		
Dessert		
Snack		
Dinner		
Dessert		

Please sign the medicine book ☐   Please provide some more:

Please sign the accident book ☐   _____

Today I slept...

Fell Asleep	Woke Up

Today my nappies were...

Time	Wet	Soiled	Dry	Checked

I had the following milk today...

Time	fl oz	Time	fl oz

Today I...

Went on the potty ☐   Went on the toilet ☐   I tried! ☐

Additional Notes...

Date

Today I have been...

Happy ☐ Chatty ☐ Quiet ☐ Sad ☐ Funny ☐ Tired ☐

Grumpy ☐ Noisy ☐ Friendly ☐ Ill ☐ Rebellious ☐ Energetic ☐

The activities I did today were...

Today I learnt about...

Today I have eaten...

Meal	What it was	All/most/some/none
Breakfast		
Snack		
Lunch		
Dessert		
Snack		
Dinner		
Dessert		

Please sign the medicine book ☐ Please provide some more:

Please sign the accident book ☐ _____

Today I slept...

Fell Asleep	Woke Up

Today my nappies were...

Time	Wet	Soiled	Dry	Checked

I had the following milk today...

Time	fl oz	Time	fl oz

Today I...

Went on the potty ☐   Went on the toilet ☐   I tried! ☐

Additional Notes...

Date (_____)

Today I have been...

Happy ☐	Chatty ☐	Quiet ☐	Sad ☐	Funny ☐	Tired ☐
Grumpy ☐	Noisy ☐	Friendly ☐	Ill ☐	Rebellious ☐	Energetic ☐

The activities I did today were...

Today I learnt about...

Today I have eaten...

Meal	What it was	All/most/some/none
Breakfast		
Snack		
Lunch		
Dessert		
Snack		
Dinner		
Dessert		

Please sign the medicine book ☐   Please provide some more:

Please sign the accident book ☐   _____

Today I slept...

Fell Asleep	Woke Up

Today my nappies were...

Time	Wet	Soiled	Dry	Checked

I had the following milk today...

Time	fl oz	Time	fl oz

Today I...

Went on the potty ☐ Went on the toilet ☐ I tried! ☐

Additional Notes...

Date ( )

Today I have been...

Happy ☐	Chatty ☐	Quiet ☐	Sad ☐	Funny ☐	Tired ☐
Grumpy ☐	Noisy ☐	Friendly ☐	Ill ☐	Rebellious ☐	Energetic ☐

The activities I did today were...

Today I learnt about...

Today I have eaten...

Meal	What it was	All/most/some/none
Breakfast		
Snack		
Lunch		
Dessert		
Snack		
Dinner		
Dessert		

Please sign the medicine book ☐ Please provide some more:

Please sign the accident book ☐ _____

Today I slept...

Fell Asleep	Woke Up

Today my nappies were...

Time	Wet	Soiled	Dry	Checked

I had the following milk today...

Time	fl oz	Time	fl oz

Today I...

Went on the potty ☐ Went on the toilet ☐ I tried! ☐

Additional Notes...

Observations

This weekend I...

Weekly Planning

	Trips	Activities	Notes
Monday			
Tuesday			
Wednesday			
Thursday			
Friday			

Parent's Notes

Monday
Tuesday
Wednesday
Thursday
Friday

Date (_____)

Today I have been...

Happy ☐	Chatty ☐	Quiet ☐	Sad ☐	Funny ☐	Tired ☐
Grumpy ☐	Noisy ☐	Friendly ☐	Ill ☐	Rebellious ☐	Energetic ☐

The activities I did today were...

Today I learnt about...

Today I have eaten...

Meal	What it was	All/most/some/none
Breakfast		
Snack		
Lunch		
Dessert		
Snack		
Dinner		
Dessert		

Please sign the medicine book ☐   Please provide some more:

Please sign the accident book ☐   _____

Today I slept...

Fell Asleep	Woke Up

Today my nappies were...

Time	Wet	Soiled	Dry	Checked

I had the following milk today...

Time	fl oz	Time	fl oz

Today I...

Went on the potty ☐ Went on the toilet ☐ I tried! ☐

Additional Notes...

Date [   ]

Today I have been...

Happy ☐ Chatty ☐ Quiet ☐ Sad ☐ Funny ☐ Tired ☐

Grumpy ☐ Noisy ☐ Friendly ☐ Ill ☐ Rebellious ☐ Energetic ☐

The activities I did today were...

[   ]

Today I learnt about...

[   ]

Today I have eaten...

Meal	What it was	All/most/some/none
Breakfast		
Snack		
Lunch		
Dessert		
Snack		
Dinner		
Dessert		

Please sign the medicine book ☐   Please provide some more:

Please sign the accident book ☐   _____

Today I slept...

Fell Asleep	Woke Up

Today my nappies were...

Time	Wet	Soiled	Dry	Checked

I had the following milk today...

Time	fl oz	Time	fl oz

Today I...

Went on the potty ☐ Went on the toilet ☐ I tried! ☐

Additional Notes...

Date (_____)

Today I have been...

Happy ☐	Chatty ☐	Quiet ☐	Sad ☐	Funny ☐	Tired ☐
Grumpy ☐	Noisy ☐	Friendly ☐	Ill ☐	Rebellious ☐	Energetic ☐

The activities I did today were...

Today I learnt about...

Today I have eaten...

Meal	What it was	All/most/some/none
Breakfast		
Snack		
Lunch		
Dessert		
Snack		
Dinner		
Dessert		

Please sign the medicine book ☐   Please provide some more:

Please sign the accident book ☐   _____

Today I slept...

Fell Asleep	Woke Up

Today my nappies were...

Time	Wet	Soiled	Dry	Checked

I had the following milk today...

Time	fl oz	Time	fl oz

Today I...

Went on the potty ☐ Went on the toilet ☐ I tried! ☐

Additional Notes...

Date [   ]

Today I have been...

Happy ☐	Chatty ☐	Quiet ☐	Sad ☐	Funny ☐	Tired ☐
Grumpy ☐	Noisy ☐	Friendly ☐	Ill ☐	Rebellious ☐	Energetic ☐

The activities I did today were...

[   ]

Today I learnt about...

[   ]

Today I have eaten...

Meal	What it was	All/most/some/none
Breakfast		
Snack		
Lunch		
Dessert		
Snack		
Dinner		
Dessert		

Please sign the medicine book ☐   Please provide some more:

Please sign the accident book ☐   _____

Today I slept...

Fell Asleep	Woke Up

Today my nappies were...

Time	Wet	Soiled	Dry	Checked

I had the following milk today...

Time	fl oz	Time	fl oz

Today I...

Went on the potty ☐ Went on the toilet ☐ I tried! ☐

Additional Notes...

Date

Today I have been...

Happy ☐ Chatty ☐ Quiet ☐ Sad ☐ Funny ☐ Tired ☐

Grumpy ☐ Noisy ☐ Friendly ☐ Ill ☐ Rebellious ☐ Energetic ☐

The activities I did today were...

Today I learnt about...

Today I have eaten...

Meal	What it was	All/most/some/none
Breakfast		
Snack		
Lunch		
Dessert		
Snack		
Dinner		
Dessert		

Please sign the medicine book ☐   Please provide some more:

Please sign the accident book ☐   _____

Today I slept...

Fell Asleep	Woke Up

Today my nappies were...

Time	Wet	Soiled	Dry	Checked

I had the following milk today...

Time	fl oz	Time	fl oz

Today I...

Went on the potty ☐   Went on the toilet ☐   I tried! ☐

Additional Notes...

Observations

This weekend I...

Weekly Planning

	Trips	Activities	Notes
Monday			
Tuesday			
Wednesday			
Thursday			
Friday			

Parent's Notes

Monday

Tuesday

Wednesday

Thursday

Friday

Date [   ]

Today I have been...

Happy ☐   Chatty ☐   Quiet ☐   Sad ☐   Funny ☐   Tired ☐

Grumpy ☐   Noisy ☐   Friendly ☐   Ill ☐   Rebellious ☐   Energetic ☐

The activities I did today were...

[   ]

Today I learnt about...

[   ]

Today I have eaten...

Meal	What it was	All/most/some/none
Breakfast		
Snack		
Lunch		
Dessert		
Snack		
Dinner		
Dessert		

Please sign the medicine book ☐   Please provide some more:

Please sign the accident book ☐   _____

Today I slept...

Fell Asleep	Woke Up

Today my nappies were...

Time	Wet	Soiled	Dry	Checked

I had the following milk today...

Time	fl oz	Time	fl oz

Today I...

Went on the potty ☐ Went on the toilet ☐ I tried! ☐

Additional Notes...

Date _____

Today I have been...

Happy ☐	Chatty ☐	Quiet ☐	Sad ☐	Funny ☐	Tired ☐
Grumpy ☐	Noisy ☐	Friendly ☐	Ill ☐	Rebellious ☐	Energetic ☐

The activities I did today were...

_____

Today I learnt about...

_____

Today I have eaten...

Meal	What it was	All/most/some/none
Breakfast		
Snack		
Lunch		
Dessert		
Snack		
Dinner		
Dessert		

Please sign the medicine book ☐   Please provide some more:

Please sign the accident book ☐   _____

Today I slept...

Fell Asleep	Woke Up

Today my nappies were...

Time	Wet	Soiled	Dry	Checked

I had the following milk today...

Time	fl oz	Time	fl oz

Today I...

Went on the potty ☐   Went on the toilet ☐   I tried! ☐

Additional Notes...

Date (_____)

Today I have been...

| Happy ☐ | Chatty ☐ | Quiet ☐ | Sad ☐ | Funny ☐ | Tired ☐ |

| Grumpy ☐ | Noisy ☐ | Friendly ☐ | Ill ☐ | Rebellious ☐ | Energetic ☐ |

The activities I did today were...

Today I learnt about...

Today I have eaten...

Meal	What it was	All/most/some/none
Breakfast		
Snack		
Lunch		
Dessert		
Snack		
Dinner		
Dessert		

Please sign the medicine book ☐   Please provide some more:

Please sign the accident book ☐   _____

Today I slept...

Fell Asleep	Woke Up

Today my nappies were...

Time	Wet	Soiled	Dry	Checked

I had the following milk today...

Time	fl oz	Time	fl oz

Today I...

Went on the potty ☐   Went on the toilet ☐   I tried! ☐

Additional Notes...

Date

Today I have been...

Happy ☐ Chatty ☐ Quiet ☐ Sad ☐ Funny ☐ Tired ☐

Grumpy ☐ Noisy ☐ Friendly ☐ Ill ☐ Rebellious ☐ Energetic ☐

The activities I did today were...

Today I learnt about...

Today I have eaten...

Meal	What it was	All/most/some/none
Breakfast		
Snack		
Lunch		
Dessert		
Snack		
Dinner		
Dessert		

Please sign the medicine book ☐   Please provide some more:

Please sign the accident book ☐   _____

Today I slept...

Fell Asleep	Woke Up

Today my nappies were...

Time	Wet	Soiled	Dry	Checked

I had the following milk today...

Time	fl oz	Time	fl oz

Today I...

Went on the potty ☐ Went on the toilet ☐ I tried! ☐

Additional Notes...

Date ⬭

Today I have been...

Happy ☐	Chatty ☐	Quiet ☐	Sad ☐	Funny ☐	Tired ☐
Grumpy ☐	Noisy ☐	Friendly ☐	Ill ☐	Rebellious ☐	Energetic ☐

The activities I did today were...

Today I learnt about...

Today I have eaten...

Meal	What it was	All/most/some/none
Breakfast		
Snack		
Lunch		
Dessert		
Snack		
Dinner		
Dessert		

Please sign the medicine book ☐   Please provide some more:

Please sign the accident book ☐   _____

Early Years Daily Diary | 47

Today I slept...

Fell Asleep	Woke Up

Today my nappies were...

Time	Wet	Soiled	Dry	Checked

I had the following milk today...

Time	fl oz	Time	fl oz

Today I...

Went on the potty ☐ Went on the toilet ☐ I tried! ☐

Additional Notes...

Observations

This weekend I...

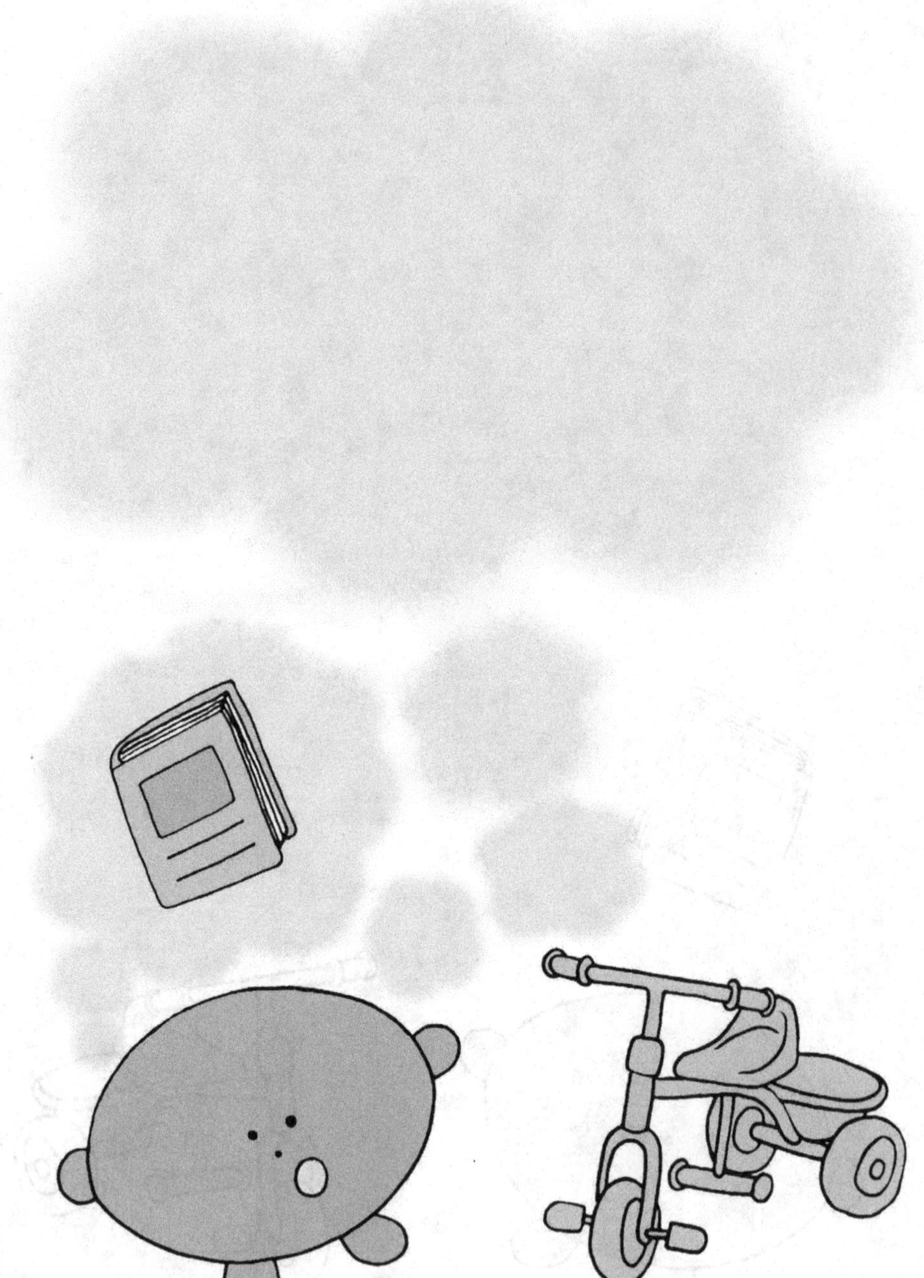

Weekly Planning

	Trips	Activities	Notes
Monday			
Tuesday			
Wednesday			
Thursday			
Friday			

Parent's Notes

Monday

Tuesday

Wednesday

Thursday

Friday

Date ( )

Today I have been...

Happy ☐	Chatty ☐	Quiet ☐	Sad ☐	Funny ☐	Tired ☐
Grumpy ☐	Noisy ☐	Friendly ☐	Ill ☐	Rebellious ☐	Energetic ☐

The activities I did today were...

Today I learnt about...

Today I have eaten...

Meal	What it was	All/most/some/none
Breakfast		
Snack		
Lunch		
Dessert		
Snack		
Dinner		
Dessert		

Please sign the medicine book ☐   Please provide some more:

Please sign the accident book ☐   _____

Today I slept...

Fell Asleep	Woke Up

Today my nappies were...

Time	Wet	Soiled	Dry	Checked

I had the following milk today...

Time	fl oz	Time	fl oz

Today I...

Went on the potty ☐   Went on the toilet ☐   I tried! ☐

Additional Notes...

Date ( )

Today I have been...

Happy ☐ Chatty ☐ Quiet ☐ Sad ☐ Funny ☐ Tired ☐

Grumpy ☐ Noisy ☐ Friendly ☐ Ill ☐ Rebellious ☐ Energetic ☐

The activities I did today were...

Today I learnt about...

Today I have eaten...

Meal	What it was	All/most/some/none
Breakfast		
Snack		
Lunch		
Dessert		
Snack		
Dinner		
Dessert		

Please sign the medicine book ☐ Please provide some more:

Please sign the accident book ☐ _____

Today I slept...

Fell Asleep	Woke Up

Today my nappies were...

Time	Wet	Soiled	Dry	Checked

I had the following milk today...

Time	fl oz	Time	fl oz

Today I...

Went on the potty ☐ Went on the toilet ☐ I tried! ☐

Additional Notes...

Date

Today I have been...

Happy ☐	Chatty ☐	Quiet ☐	Sad ☐	Funny ☐	Tired ☐
Grumpy ☐	Noisy ☐	Friendly ☐	Ill ☐	Rebellious ☐	Energetic ☐

The activities I did today were...

Today I learnt about...

Today I have eaten...

Meal	What it was	All/most/some/none
Breakfast		
Snack		
Lunch		
Dessert		
Snack		
Dinner		
Dessert		

Please sign the medicine book ☐   Please provide some more:

Please sign the accident book ☐   _____

Today I slept...

Fell Asleep	Woke Up

Today my nappies were...

Time	Wet	Soiled	Dry	Checked

I had the following milk today...

Time	fl oz	Time	fl oz

Today I...

Went on the potty ☐   Went on the toilet ☐   I tried! ☐

Additional Notes...

Date

Today I have been...

Happy ☐   Chatty ☐   Quiet ☐   Sad ☐   Funny ☐   Tired ☐

Grumpy ☐   Noisy ☐   Friendly ☐   Ill ☐   Rebellious ☐   Energetic ☐

The activities I did today were...

Today I learnt about...

Today I have eaten...

Meal	What it was	All/most/some/none
Breakfast		
Snack		
Lunch		
Dessert		
Snack		
Dinner		
Dessert		

Please sign the medicine book ☐   Please provide some more:

Please sign the accident book ☐   _____

Today I slept...

Fell Asleep	Woke Up

Today my nappies were...

Time	Wet	Soiled	Dry	Checked

I had the following milk today...

Time	fl oz	Time	fl oz

Today I...

Went on the potty ☐ Went on the toilet ☐ I tried! ☐

Additional Notes...

Date (   )

Today I have been...

| Happy ☐ | Chatty ☐ | Quiet ☐ | Sad ☐ | Funny ☐ | Tired ☐ |
| Grumpy ☐ | Noisy ☐ | Friendly ☐ | Ill ☐ | Rebellious ☐ | Energetic ☐ |

The activities I did today were...

Today I learnt about...

Today I have eaten...

Meal	What it was	All/most/some/none
Breakfast		
Snack		
Lunch		
Dessert		
Snack		
Dinner		
Dessert		

Please sign the medicine book ☐   Please provide some more:

Please sign the accident book ☐   _____

Today I slept...

Fell Asleep	Woke Up

Today my nappies were...

Time	Wet	Soiled	Dry	Checked

I had the following milk today...

Time	fl oz	Time	fl oz

Today I...

Went on the potty ☐ Went on the toilet ☐ I tried! ☐

Additional Notes...

Observations

This weekend I...

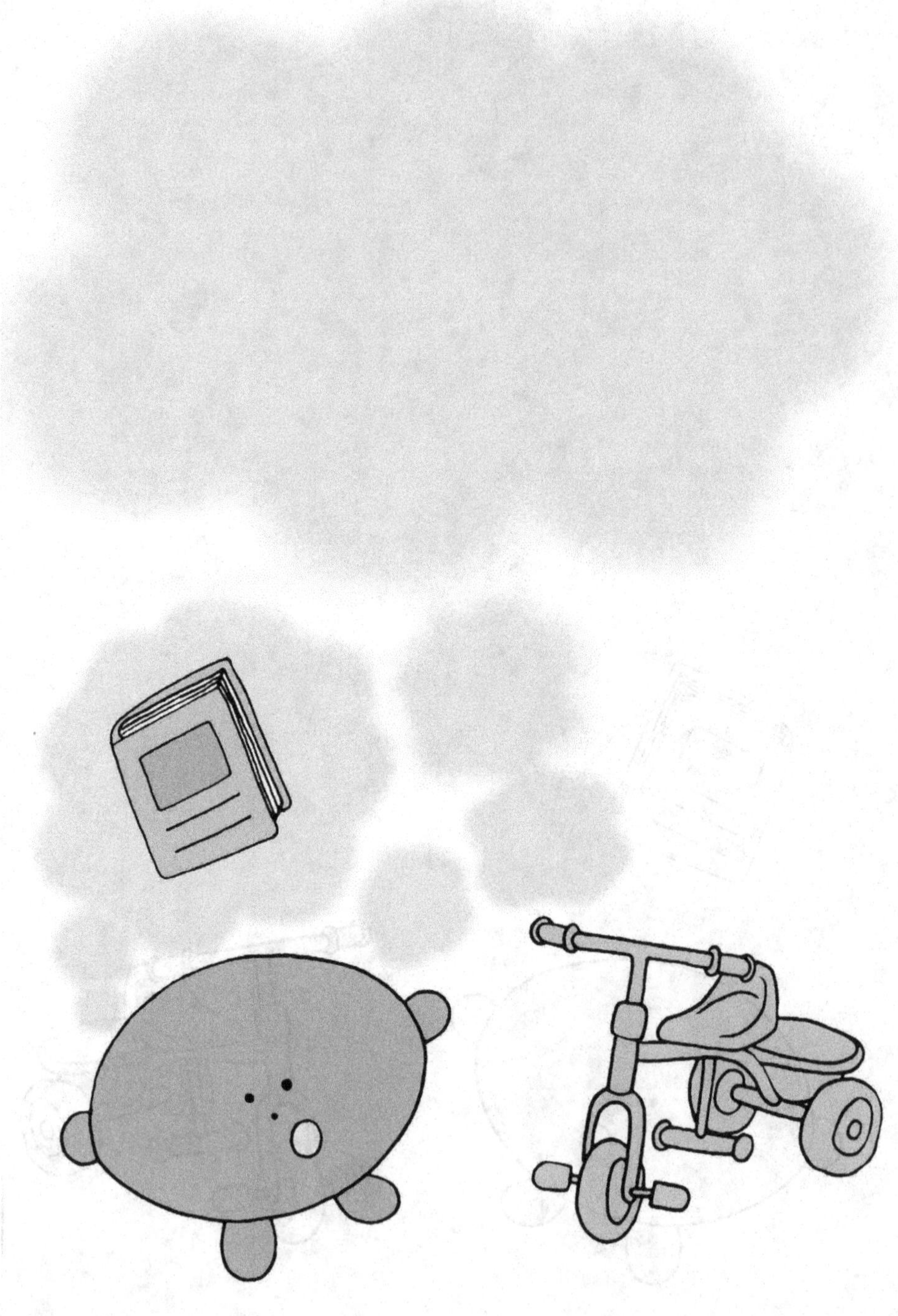

Weekly Planning

	Trips	Activities	Notes
Monday			
Tuesday			
Wednesday			
Thursday			
Friday			

Parent's Notes

Monday

Tuesday

Wednesday

Thursday

Friday

Date ( )

Today I have been...

Happy ☐	Chatty ☐	Quiet ☐	Sad ☐	Funny ☐	Tired ☐
Grumpy ☐	Noisy ☐	Friendly ☐	Ill ☐	Rebellious ☐	Energetic ☐

The activities I did today were...

Today I learnt about...

Today I have eaten...

Meal	What it was	All/most/some/none
Breakfast		
Snack		
Lunch		
Dessert		
Snack		
Dinner		
Dessert		

Please sign the medicine book ☐ Please provide some more:

Please sign the accident book ☐ _____

Today I slept...

Fell Asleep	Woke Up

Today my nappies were...

Time	Wet	Soiled	Dry	Checked

I had the following milk today...

Time	fl oz	Time	fl oz

Today I...

Went on the potty ☐   Went on the toilet ☐   I tried! ☐

Additional Notes...

Date ⬭

Today I have been...

Happy ☐	Chatty ☐	Quiet ☐	Sad ☐	Funny ☐	Tired ☐
Grumpy ☐	Noisy ☐	Friendly ☐	Ill ☐	Rebellious ☐	Energetic ☐

The activities I did today were...

Today I learnt about...

Today I have eaten...

Meal	What it was	All/most/some/none
Breakfast		
Snack		
Lunch		
Dessert		
Snack		
Dinner		
Dessert		

Please sign the medicine book ☐   Please provide some more:

Please sign the accident book ☐   _____

Today I slept...

Fell Asleep	Woke Up

Today my nappies were...

Time	Wet	Soiled	Dry	Checked

I had the following milk today...

Time	fl oz	Time	fl oz

Today I...

Went on the potty ☐   Went on the toilet ☐   I tried! ☐

Additional Notes...

Date ⬭

Today I have been...

Happy ☐ Chatty ☐ Quiet ☐ Sad ☐ Funny ☐ Tired ☐

Grumpy ☐ Noisy ☐ Friendly ☐ Ill ☐ Rebellious ☐ Energetic ☐

The activities I did today were...

Today I learnt about...

Today I have eaten...

Meal	What it was	All/most/some/none
Breakfast		
Snack		
Lunch		
Dessert		
Snack		
Dinner		
Dessert		

Please sign the medicine book ☐   Please provide some more:

Please sign the accident book ☐   _____

Today I slept...

Fell Asleep	Woke Up

Today my nappies were...

Time	Wet	Soiled	Dry	Checked

I had the following milk today...

Time	fl oz	Time	fl oz

Today I...

Went on the potty ☐ Went on the toilet ☐ I tried! ☐

Additional Notes...

Date

Today I have been...

Happy ☐ Chatty ☐ Quiet ☐ Sad ☐ Funny ☐ Tired ☐

Grumpy ☐ Noisy ☐ Friendly ☐ Ill ☐ Rebellious ☐ Energetic ☐

The activities I did today were...

Today I learnt about...

Today I have eaten...

Meal	What it was	All/most/some/none
Breakfast		
Snack		
Lunch		
Dessert		
Snack		
Dinner		
Dessert		

Please sign the medicine book ☐   Please provide some more:

Please sign the accident book ☐   _____

Today I slept...

Fell Asleep	Woke Up

Today my nappies were...

Time	Wet	Soiled	Dry	Checked

I had the following milk today...

Time	fl oz	Time	fl oz

Today I...

Went on the potty ☐   Went on the toilet ☐   I tried! ☐

Additional Notes...

Date ( )

Today I have been...

Happy ☐ Chatty ☐ Quiet ☐ Sad ☐ Funny ☐ Tired ☐

Grumpy ☐ Noisy ☐ Friendly ☐ Ill ☐ Rebellious ☐ Energetic ☐

The activities I did today were...

[ ]

Today I learnt about...

[ ]

Today I have eaten...

Meal	What it was	All/most/some/none
Breakfast		
Snack		
Lunch		
Dessert		
Snack		
Dinner		
Dessert		

Please sign the medicine book ☐ Please provide some more:

Please sign the accident book ☐ _____

Today I slept...

Fell Asleep	Woke Up

Today my nappies were...

Time	Wet	Soiled	Dry	Checked

I had the following milk today...

Time	fl oz	Time	fl oz

Today I...

Went on the potty ☐   Went on the toilet ☐   I tried! ☐

Additional Notes...

Observations

This weekend I...

Weekly Planning

	Trips	Activities	Notes
Monday			
Tuesday			
Wednesday			
Thursday			
Friday			

Parent's Notes

Monday

Tuesday

Wednesday

Thursday

Friday

Date [   ]

Today I have been...

Happy ☐	Chatty ☐	Quiet ☐	Sad ☐	Funny ☐	Tired ☐

Grumpy ☐	Noisy ☐	Friendly ☐	Ill ☐	Rebellious ☐	Energetic ☐

The activities I did today were...

[   ]

Today I learnt about...

[   ]

Today I have eaten...

Meal	What it was	All/most/some/none
Breakfast		
Snack		
Lunch		
Dessert		
Snack		
Dinner		
Dessert		

Please sign the medicine book ☐   Please provide some more:

Please sign the accident book ☐   _____

Today I slept...

Fell Asleep	Woke Up

Today my nappies were...

Time	Wet	Soiled	Dry	Checked

I had the following milk today...

Time	fl oz	Time	fl oz

Today I...

Went on the potty ☐   Went on the toilet ☐   I tried! ☐

Additional Notes...

Date ( )

Today I have been...

Happy ☐	Chatty ☐	Quiet ☐	Sad ☐	Funny ☐	Tired ☐
Grumpy ☐	Noisy ☐	Friendly ☐	Ill ☐	Rebellious ☐	Energetic ☐

The activities I did today were...

Today I learnt about...

Today I have eaten...

Meal	What it was	All/most/some/none
Breakfast		
Snack		
Lunch		
Dessert		
Snack		
Dinner		
Dessert		

Please sign the medicine book ☐   Please provide some more:

Please sign the accident book ☐   _____

Today I slept...

Fell Asleep	Woke Up

Today my nappies were...

Time	Wet	Soiled	Dry	Checked

I had the following milk today...

Time	fl oz	Time	fl oz

Today I...

Went on the potty ☐ Went on the toilet ☐ I tried! ☐

Additional Notes...

Date

Today I have been...

Happy ☐ Chatty ☐ Quiet ☐ Sad ☐ Funny ☐ Tired ☐

Grumpy ☐ Noisy ☐ Friendly ☐ Ill ☐ Rebellious ☐ Energetic ☐

The activities I did today were...

Today I learnt about...

Today I have eaten...

Meal	What it was	All/most/some/none
Breakfast		
Snack		
Lunch		
Dessert		
Snack		
Dinner		
Dessert		

Please sign the medicine book ☐   Please provide some more:

Please sign the accident book ☐   _____

Today I slept...

Fell Asleep	Woke Up

Today my nappies were...

Time	Wet	Soiled	Dry	Checked

I had the following milk today...

Time	fl oz	Time	fl oz

Today I...

Went on the potty ☐ Went on the toilet ☐ I tried! ☐

Additional Notes...

Date ( )

Today I have been...

Happy ☐	Chatty ☐	Quiet ☐	Sad ☐	Funny ☐	Tired ☐

Grumpy ☐	Noisy ☐	Friendly ☐	Ill ☐	Rebellious ☐	Energetic ☐

The activities I did today were...

Today I learnt about...

Today I have eaten...

Meal	What it was	All/most/some/none
Breakfast		
Snack		
Lunch		
Dessert		
Snack		
Dinner		
Dessert		

Please sign the medicine book ☐   Please provide some more:

Please sign the accident book ☐   _____

Today I slept...

Fell Asleep	Woke Up

Today my nappies were...

Time	Wet	Soiled	Dry	Checked

I had the following milk today...

Time	fl oz	Time	fl oz

Today I...

Went on the potty ☐   Went on the toilet ☐   I tried! ☐

Additional Notes...

Date ( )

Today I have been...

| Happy ☐ | Chatty ☐ | Quiet ☐ | Sad ☐ | Funny ☐ | Tired ☐ |

| Grumpy ☐ | Noisy ☐ | Friendly ☐ | Ill ☐ | Rebellious ☐ | Energetic ☐ |

The activities I did today were...

Today I learnt about...

Today I have eaten...

Meal	What it was	All/most/some/none
Breakfast		
Snack		
Lunch		
Dessert		
Snack		
Dinner		
Dessert		

Please sign the medicine book ☐   Please provide some more:

Please sign the accident book ☐   _____

Today I slept...

Fell Asleep	Woke Up

Today my nappies were...

Time	Wet	Soiled	Dry	Checked

I had the following milk today...

Time	fl oz	Time	fl oz

Today I...

Went on the potty ☐   Went on the toilet ☐   I tried! ☐

Additional Notes...

Observations

This weekend I...

Weekly Planning

	Trips	Activities	Notes
Monday			
Tuesday			
Wednesday			
Thursday			
Friday			

Parent's Notes

Monday

Tuesday

Wednesday

Thursday

Friday

Date [   ]

Today I have been...

Happy ☐	Chatty ☐	Quiet ☐	Sad ☐	Funny ☐	Tired ☐
Grumpy ☐	Noisy ☐	Friendly ☐	Ill ☐	Rebellious ☐	Energetic ☐

The activities I did today were...

[   ]

Today I learnt about...

[   ]

Today I have eaten...

Meal	What it was	All/most/some/none
Breakfast		
Snack		
Lunch		
Dessert		
Snack		
Dinner		
Dessert		

Please sign the medicine book ☐   Please provide some more:

Please sign the accident book ☐   _____

Today I slept...

Fell Asleep	Woke Up

Today my nappies were...

Time	Wet	Soiled	Dry	Checked

I had the following milk today...

Time	fl oz	Time	fl oz

Today I...

Went on the potty ☐   Went on the toilet ☐   I tried! ☐

Additional Notes...

Date ( )

Today I have been...

Happy ☐	Chatty ☐	Quiet ☐	Sad ☐	Funny ☐	Tired ☐
Grumpy ☐	Noisy ☐	Friendly ☐	Ill ☐	Rebellious ☐	Energetic ☐

The activities I did today were...

Today I learnt about...

Today I have eaten...

Meal	What it was	All/most/some/none
Breakfast		
Snack		
Lunch		
Dessert		
Snack		
Dinner		
Dessert		

Please sign the medicine book ☐   Please provide some more:

Please sign the accident book ☐   _____

Today I slept...

Fell Asleep	Woke Up

Today my nappies were...

Time	Wet	Soiled	Dry	Checked

I had the following milk today...

Time	fl oz	Time	fl oz

Today I...

 Went on the potty ☐   Went on the toilet ☐   I tried! ☐

Additional Notes...

Date

Today I have been...

Happy ☐ Chatty ☐ Quiet ☐ Sad ☐ Funny ☐ Tired ☐

Grumpy ☐ Noisy ☐ Friendly ☐ Ill ☐ Rebellious ☐ Energetic ☐

The activities I did today were...

Today I learnt about...

Today I have eaten...

Meal	What it was	All/most/some/none
Breakfast		
Snack		
Lunch		
Dessert		
Snack		
Dinner		
Dessert		

Please sign the medicine book ☐   Please provide some more:

Please sign the accident book ☐   _____

Today I slept...

Fell Asleep	Woke Up

Today my nappies were...

Time	Wet	Soiled	Dry	Checked

I had the following milk today...

Time	fl oz	Time	fl oz

Today I...

Went on the potty ☐   Went on the toilet ☐   I tried! ☐

Additional Notes...

Date

Today I have been...

Happy ☐	Chatty ☐	Quiet ☐	Sad ☐	Funny ☐	Tired ☐
Grumpy ☐	Noisy ☐	Friendly ☐	Ill ☐	Rebellious ☐	Energetic ☐

The activities I did today were...

Today I learnt about...

Today I have eaten...

Meal	What it was	All/most/some/none
Breakfast		
Snack		
Lunch		
Dessert		
Snack		
Dinner		
Dessert		

Please sign the medicine book ☐   Please provide some more:

Please sign the accident book ☐   _____

Today I slept...

Fell Asleep	Woke Up

Today my nappies were...

Time	Wet	Soiled	Dry	Checked

I had the following milk today...

Time	fl oz	Time	fl oz

Today I...

Went on the potty ☐ Went on the toilet ☐ I tried! ☐

Additional Notes...

Date

Today I have been...

Happy ☐	Chatty ☐	Quiet ☐	Sad ☐	Funny ☐	Tired ☐
Grumpy ☐	Noisy ☐	Friendly ☐	Ill ☐	Rebellious ☐	Energetic ☐

The activities I did today were...

Today I learnt about...

Today I have eaten...

Meal	What it was	All/most/some/none
Breakfast		
Snack		
Lunch		
Dessert		
Snack		
Dinner		
Dessert		

Please sign the medicine book ☐   Please provide some more:

Please sign the accident book ☐   _____

Today I slept...

Fell Asleep	Woke Up

Today my nappies were...

Time	Wet	Soiled	Dry	Checked

I had the following milk today...

Time	fl oz	Time	fl oz

Today I...

Went on the potty ☐   Went on the toilet ☐   I tried! ☐

Additional Notes...

Observations

This weekend I...

Weekly Planning

	Trips	Activities	Notes
Monday			
Tuesday			
Wednesday			
Thursday			
Friday			

Parent's Notes

Monday

Tuesday

Wednesday

Thursday

Friday

Date ⟨＿＿＿＿＿＿＿＿＿＿⟩

Today I have been...

Happy ☐	Chatty ☐	Quiet ☐	Sad ☐	Funny ☐	Tired ☐
Grumpy ☐	Noisy ☐	Friendly ☐	Ill ☐	Rebellious ☐	Energetic ☐

The activities I did today were...

Today I learnt about...

Today I have eaten...

Meal	What it was	All/most/some/none
Breakfast		
Snack		
Lunch		
Dessert		
Snack		
Dinner		
Dessert		

Please sign the medicine book ☐ Please provide some more:

Please sign the accident book ☐ ＿＿＿＿＿＿＿＿＿＿＿＿＿

Today I slept...

Fell Asleep	Woke Up

Today my nappies were...

Time	Wet	Soiled	Dry	Checked

I had the following milk today...

Time	fl oz	Time	fl oz

Today I...

Went on the potty ☐ Went on the toilet ☐ I tried! ☐

Additional Notes...

Date ⬭

Today I have been...

| Happy ☐ | Chatty ☐ | Quiet ☐ | Sad ☐ | Funny ☐ | Tired ☐ |

| Grumpy ☐ | Noisy ☐ | Friendly ☐ | Ill ☐ | Rebellious ☐ | Energetic ☐ |

The activities I did today were...

Today I learnt about...

Today I have eaten...

Meal	What it was	All/most/some/none
Breakfast		
Snack		
Lunch		
Dessert		
Snack		
Dinner		
Dessert		

Please sign the medicine book ☐   Please provide some more:

Please sign the accident book ☐   _____

Today I slept...

Fell Asleep	Woke Up

Today my nappies were...

Time	Wet	Soiled	Dry	Checked

I had the following milk today...

Time	fl oz	Time	fl oz

Today I...

Went on the potty ☐   Went on the toilet ☐   I tried! ☐

Additional Notes...

Date (   )

Today I have been...

Happy ☐ Chatty ☐ Quiet ☐ Sad ☐ Funny ☐ Tired ☐

Grumpy ☐ Noisy ☐ Friendly ☐ Ill ☐ Rebellious ☐ Energetic ☐

The activities I did today were...

Today I learnt about...

Today I have eaten...

Meal	What it was	All/most/some/none
Breakfast		
Snack		
Lunch		
Dessert		
Snack		
Dinner		
Dessert		

Please sign the medicine book ☐   Please provide some more:

Please sign the accident book ☐   _____

Today I slept...

Fell Asleep	Woke Up

Today my nappies were...

Time	Wet	Soiled	Dry	Checked

I had the following milk today...

Time	fl oz	Time	fl oz

Today I...

Went on the potty ☐ Went on the toilet ☐ I tried! ☐

Additional Notes...

Date ( )

Today I have been...

Happy ☐ Chatty ☐ Quiet ☐ Sad ☐ Funny ☐ Tired ☐

Grumpy ☐ Noisy ☐ Friendly ☐ Ill ☐ Rebellious ☐ Energetic ☐

The activities I did today were...

Today I learnt about...

Today I have eaten...

Meal	What it was	All/most/some/none
Breakfast		
Snack		
Lunch		
Dessert		
Snack		
Dinner		
Dessert		

Please sign the medicine book ☐ Please provide some more:

Please sign the accident book ☐ _____

Today I slept...

Fell Asleep	Woke Up

Today my nappies were...

Time	Wet	Soiled	Dry	Checked

I had the following milk today...

Time	fl oz	Time	fl oz

Today I...

Went on the potty ☐   Went on the toilet ☐   I tried! ☐

Additional Notes...

Date ⬭

Today I have been...

Happy ☐ Chatty ☐ Quiet ☐ Sad ☐ Funny ☐ Tired ☐

Grumpy ☐ Noisy ☐ Friendly ☐ Ill ☐ Rebellious ☐ Energetic ☐

The activities I did today were...

Today I learnt about...

Today I have eaten...

Meal	What it was	All/most/some/none
Breakfast		
Snack		
Lunch		
Dessert		
Snack		
Dinner		
Dessert		

Please sign the medicine book ☐ Please provide some more:

Please sign the accident book ☐ _____

Today I slept...

Fell Asleep	Woke Up

Today my nappies were...

Time	Wet	Soiled	Dry	Checked

I had the following milk today...

Time	fl oz	Time	fl oz

Today I...

Went on the potty ☐   Went on the toilet ☐   I tried! ☐

Additional Notes...

Observations

This weekend I...

Weekly Planning

	Trips	Activities	Notes
Monday			
Tuesday			
Wednesday			
Thursday			
Friday			

Parent's Notes

Monday

Tuesday

Wednesday

Thursday

Friday

Date ⬭

Today I have been...

| Happy ☐ | Chatty ☐ | Quiet ☐ | Sad ☐ | Funny ☐ | Tired ☐ |

| Grumpy ☐ | Noisy ☐ | Friendly ☐ | Ill ☐ | Rebellious ☐ | Energetic ☐ |

The activities I did today were...

Today I learnt about...

Today I have eaten...

Meal	What it was	All/most/some/none
Breakfast		
Snack		
Lunch		
Dessert		
Snack		
Dinner		
Dessert		

Please sign the medicine book ☐   Please provide some more:

Please sign the accident book ☐   _____

Today I slept...

Fell Asleep	Woke Up

Today my nappies were...

Time	Wet	Soiled	Dry	Checked

I had the following milk today...

Time	fl oz	Time	fl oz

Today I...

Went on the potty ☐   Went on the toilet ☐   I tried! ☐

Additional Notes...

Date (_____)

Today I have been...

Happy ☐ Chatty ☐ Quiet ☐ Sad ☐ Funny ☐ Tired ☐

Grumpy ☐ Noisy ☐ Friendly ☐ Ill ☐ Rebellious ☐ Energetic ☐

The activities I did today were...

Today I learnt about...

Today I have eaten...

Meal	What it was	All/most/some/none
Breakfast		
Snack		
Lunch		
Dessert		
Snack		
Dinner		
Dessert		

Please sign the medicine book ☐   Please provide some more:

Please sign the accident book ☐   _____

Today I slept...

Fell Asleep	Woke Up

Today my nappies were...

Time	Wet	Soiled	Dry	Checked

I had the following milk today...

Time	fl oz	Time	fl oz

Today I...

Went on the potty ☐   Went on the toilet ☐   I tried! ☐

Additional Notes...

Date

Today I have been...

Happy ☐ Chatty ☐ Quiet ☐ Sad ☐ Funny ☐ Tired ☐

Grumpy ☐ Noisy ☐ Friendly ☐ Ill ☐ Rebellious ☐ Energetic ☐

The activities I did today were...

Today I learnt about...

Today I have eaten...

Meal	What it was	All/most/some/none
Breakfast		
Snack		
Lunch		
Dessert		
Snack		
Dinner		
Dessert		

Please sign the medicine book ☐   Please provide some more:

Please sign the accident book ☐   _____

Today I slept...

Fell Asleep	Woke Up

Today my nappies were...

Time	Wet	Soiled	Dry	Checked

I had the following milk today...

Time	fl oz	Time	fl oz

Today I...

Went on the potty ☐ Went on the toilet ☐ I tried! ☐

Additional Notes...

Date

Today I have been...

Happy ☐ Chatty ☐ Quiet ☐ Sad ☐ Funny ☐ Tired ☐

Grumpy ☐ Noisy ☐ Friendly ☐ Ill ☐ Rebellious ☐ Energetic ☐

The activities I did today were...

Today I learnt about...

Today I have eaten...

Meal	What it was	All/most/some/none
Breakfast		
Snack		
Lunch		
Dessert		
Snack		
Dinner		
Dessert		

Please sign the medicine book ☐   Please provide some more:

Please sign the accident book ☐   _____

Today I slept...

Fell Asleep	Woke Up

Today my nappies were...

Time	Wet	Soiled	Dry	Checked

I had the following milk today...

Time	fl oz	Time	fl oz

Today I...

Went on the potty ☐　Went on the toilet ☐　I tried! ☐

Additional Notes...

Date (   )

Today I have been...

Happy ☐ Chatty ☐ Quiet ☐ Sad ☐ Funny ☐ Tired ☐

Grumpy ☐ Noisy ☐ Friendly ☐ Ill ☐ Rebellious ☐ Energetic ☐

The activities I did today were...

Today I learnt about...

Today I have eaten...

Meal	What it was	All/most/some/none
Breakfast		
Snack		
Lunch		
Dessert		
Snack		
Dinner		
Dessert		

Please sign the medicine book ☐ Please provide some more:

Please sign the accident book ☐ _____

Today I slept...

Fell Asleep	Woke Up

Today my nappies were...

Time	Wet	Soiled	Dry	Checked

I had the following milk today...

Time	fl oz	Time	fl oz

Today I...

Went on the potty ☐   Went on the toilet ☐   I tried! ☐

Additional Notes...

Observations

This weekend I...

Weekly Planning

	Trips	Activities	Notes
Monday			
Tuesday			
Wednesday			
Thursday			
Friday			

Parent's Notes

Monday

Tuesday

Wednesday

Thursday

Friday

Date

Today I have been...

Happy ☐   Chatty ☐   Quiet ☐   Sad ☐   Funny ☐   Tired ☐

Grumpy ☐   Noisy ☐   Friendly ☐   Ill ☐   Rebellious ☐   Energetic ☐

The activities I did today were...

Today I learnt about...

Today I have eaten...

Meal	What it was	All/most/some/none
Breakfast		
Snack		
Lunch		
Dessert		
Snack		
Dinner		
Dessert		

Please sign the medicine book ☐   Please provide some more:

Please sign the accident book ☐   _____

Today I slept...

Fell Asleep	Woke Up

Today my nappies were...

Time	Wet	Soiled	Dry	Checked

I had the following milk today...

Time	fl oz	Time	fl oz

Today I...

Went on the potty ☐   Went on the toilet ☐   I tried! ☐

Additional Notes...

Date ⬚

Today I have been...

| Happy ☐ | Chatty ☐ | Quiet ☐ | Sad ☐ | Funny ☐ | Tired ☐ |

| Grumpy ☐ | Noisy ☐ | Friendly ☐ | Ill ☐ | Rebellious ☐ | Energetic ☐ |

The activities I did today were...

Today I learnt about...

Today I have eaten...

Meal	What it was	All/most/some/none
Breakfast		
Snack		
Lunch		
Dessert		
Snack		
Dinner		
Dessert		

Please sign the medicine book ☐   Please provide some more:

Please sign the accident book ☐   _____

Today I slept...

Fell Asleep	Woke Up

Today my nappies were...

Time	Wet	Soiled	Dry	Checked

I had the following milk today...

Time	fl oz	Time	fl oz

Today I...

Went on the potty ☐   Went on the toilet ☐   I tried! ☐

Additional Notes...

Date ⟨_____⟩

Today I have been...

| Happy ☐ | Chatty ☐ | Quiet ☐ | Sad ☐ | Funny ☐ | Tired ☐ |

| Grumpy ☐ | Noisy ☐ | Friendly ☐ | Ill ☐ | Rebellious ☐ | Energetic ☐ |

The activities I did today were...

⟨ ⟩

Today I learnt about...

⟨ ⟩

Today I have eaten...

Meal	What it was	All/most/some/none
Breakfast		
Snack		
Lunch		
Dessert		
Snack		
Dinner		
Dessert		

Please sign the medicine book ☐ Please provide some more:

Please sign the accident book ☐ _____

Today I slept...

Fell Asleep	Woke Up

Today my nappies were...

Time	Wet	Soiled	Dry	Checked

I had the following milk today...

Time	fl oz	Time	fl oz

Today I...

Went on the potty ☐   Went on the toilet ☐   I tried! ☐

Additional Notes...

Date

Today I have been...

Happy ☐   Chatty ☐   Quiet ☐   Sad ☐   Funny ☐   Tired ☐

Grumpy ☐   Noisy ☐   Friendly ☐   Ill ☐   Rebellious ☐   Energetic ☐

The activities I did today were...

Today I learnt about...

Today I have eaten...

Meal	What it was	All/most/some/none
Breakfast		
Snack		
Lunch		
Dessert		
Snack		
Dinner		
Dessert		

Please sign the medicine book ☐   Please provide some more:

Please sign the accident book ☐   _____

Today I slept...

Fell Asleep	Woke Up

Today my nappies were...

Time	Wet	Soiled	Dry	Checked

I had the following milk today...

Time	fl oz	Time	fl oz

Today I...

Went on the potty ☐   Went on the toilet ☐   I tried! ☐

Additional Notes...

Date ( )

Today I have been...

Happy ☐ Chatty ☐ Quiet ☐ Sad ☐ Funny ☐ Tired ☐

Grumpy ☐ Noisy ☐ Friendly ☐ Ill ☐ Rebellious ☐ Energetic ☐

The activities I did today were...

Today I learnt about...

Today I have eaten...

Meal	What it was	All/most/some/none
Breakfast		
Snack		
Lunch		
Dessert		
Snack		
Dinner		
Dessert		

Please sign the medicine book ☐   Please provide some more:

Please sign the accident book ☐   _____

Today I slept...

Fell Asleep	Woke Up

Today my nappies were...

Time	Wet	Soiled	Dry	Checked

I had the following milk today...

Time	fl oz	Time	fl oz

Today I...

Went on the potty ☐   Went on the toilet ☐   I tried! ☐

Additional Notes...

Observations

This weekend I...

Weekly Planning

	Trips	Activities	Notes
Monday			
Tuesday			
Wednesday			
Thursday			
Friday			

Parent's Notes

Monday

Tuesday

Wednesday

Thursday

Friday

Date ⬭

Today I have been...

Happy ☐ Chatty ☐ Quiet ☐ Sad ☐ Funny ☐ Tired ☐

Grumpy ☐ Noisy ☐ Friendly ☐ Ill ☐ Rebellious ☐ Energetic ☐

The activities I did today were...

Today I learnt about...

Today I have eaten...

Meal	What it was	All/most/some/none
Breakfast		
Snack		
Lunch		
Dessert		
Snack		
Dinner		
Dessert		

Please sign the medicine book ☐ Please provide some more:

Please sign the accident book ☐ _____

Today I slept...

Fell Asleep	Woke Up

Today my nappies were...

Time	Wet	Soiled	Dry	Checked

I had the following milk today...

Time	fl oz	Time	fl oz

Today I...

Went on the potty ☐ Went on the toilet ☐ I tried! ☐

Additional Notes...

Date ( )

Today I have been...

Happy ☐	Chatty ☐	Quiet ☐	Sad ☐	Funny ☐	Tired ☐
Grumpy ☐	Noisy ☐	Friendly ☐	Ill ☐	Rebellious ☐	Energetic ☐

The activities I did today were...

Today I learnt about...

Today I have eaten...

Meal	What it was	All/most/some/none
Breakfast		
Snack		
Lunch		
Dessert		
Snack		
Dinner		
Dessert		

Please sign the medicine book ☐   Please provide some more:

Please sign the accident book ☐   _____

Today I slept...

Fell Asleep	Woke Up

Today my nappies were...

Time	Wet	Soiled	Dry	Checked

I had the following milk today...

Time	fl oz	Time	fl oz

Today I...

Went on the potty ☐   Went on the toilet ☐   I tried! ☐

Additional Notes...

Date _____

Today I have been...

Happy ☐ Chatty ☐ Quiet ☐ Sad ☐ Funny ☐ Tired ☐

Grumpy ☐ Noisy ☐ Friendly ☐ Ill ☐ Rebellious ☐ Energetic ☐

The activities I did today were...

Today I learnt about...

Today I have eaten...

Meal	What it was	All/most/some/none
Breakfast		
Snack		
Lunch		
Dessert		
Snack		
Dinner		
Dessert		

Please sign the medicine book ☐   Please provide some more:

Please sign the accident book ☐   _____

Today I slept...

Fell Asleep	Woke Up

Today my nappies were...

Time	Wet	Soiled	Dry	Checked

I had the following milk today...

Time	fl oz	Time	fl oz

Today I...

Went on the potty ☐   Went on the toilet ☐   I tried! ☐

Additional Notes...

Date ⬭

Today I have been...

Happy ☐	Chatty ☐	Quiet ☐	Sad ☐	Funny ☐	Tired ☐
Grumpy ☐	Noisy ☐	Friendly ☐	Ill ☐	Rebellious ☐	Energetic ☐

The activities I did today were...

Today I learnt about...

Today I have eaten...

Meal	What it was	All/most/some/none
Breakfast		
Snack		
Lunch		
Dessert		
Snack		
Dinner		
Dessert		

Please sign the medicine book ☐   Please provide some more:

Please sign the accident book ☐   _____

Today I slept...

Fell Asleep	Woke Up

Today my nappies were...

Time	Wet	Soiled	Dry	Checked

I had the following milk today...

Time	fl oz	Time	fl oz

Today I...

Went on the potty ☐   Went on the toilet ☐   I tried! ☐

Additional Notes...

Date (_____)

Today I have been...

Happy ☐   Chatty ☐   Quiet ☐   Sad ☐   Funny ☐   Tired ☐

Grumpy ☐   Noisy ☐   Friendly ☐   Ill ☐   Rebellious ☐   Energetic ☐

The activities I did today were...

Today I learnt about...

Today I have eaten...

Meal	What it was	All/most/some/none
Breakfast		
Snack		
Lunch		
Dessert		
Snack		
Dinner		
Dessert		

Please sign the medicine book ☐   Please provide some more:

Please sign the accident book ☐   _____

Today I slept...

Fell Asleep	Woke Up

Today my nappies were...

Time	Wet	Soiled	Dry	Checked

I had the following milk today...

Time	fl oz	Time	fl oz

Today I...

Went on the potty ☐   Went on the toilet ☐   I tried! ☐

Additional Notes...

Observations

This weekend I...

Weekly Planning

	Trips	Activities	Notes
Monday			
Tuesday			
Wednesday			
Thursday			
Friday			

Parent's Notes

Monday

Tuesday

Wednesday

Thursday

Friday

Date ( )

Today I have been...

| Happy ☐ | Chatty ☐ | Quiet ☐ | Sad ☐ | Funny ☐ | Tired ☐ |

| Grumpy ☐ | Noisy ☐ | Friendly ☐ | Ill ☐ | Rebellious ☐ | Energetic ☐ |

The activities I did today were...

Today I learnt about...

Today I have eaten...

Meal	What it was	All/most/some/none
Breakfast		
Snack		
Lunch		
Dessert		
Snack		
Dinner		
Dessert		

Please sign the medicine book ☐   Please provide some more:

Please sign the accident book ☐   _____

Today I slept...

Fell Asleep	Woke Up

Today my nappies were...

Time	Wet	Soiled	Dry	Checked

I had the following milk today...

Time	fl oz	Time	fl oz

Today I...

Went on the potty ☐   Went on the toilet ☐   I tried! ☐

Additional Notes...

Date ⬭

Today I have been...

Happy ☐ Chatty ☐ Quiet ☐ Sad ☐ Funny ☐ Tired ☐

Grumpy ☐ Noisy ☐ Friendly ☐ Ill ☐ Rebellious ☐ Energetic ☐

The activities I did today were...

Today I learnt about...

Today I have eaten...

Meal	What it was	All/most/some/none
Breakfast		
Snack		
Lunch		
Dessert		
Snack		
Dinner		
Dessert		

Please sign the medicine book ☐   Please provide some more:

Please sign the accident book ☐   _____

Today I slept...

Fell Asleep	Woke Up

Today my nappies were...

Time	Wet	Soiled	Dry	Checked

I had the following milk today...

Time	fl oz	Time	fl oz

Today I...

Went on the potty ☐   Went on the toilet ☐   I tried! ☐

Additional Notes...

Date (_____)

Today I have been...

Happy ☐ Chatty ☐ Quiet ☐ Sad ☐ Funny ☐ Tired ☐

Grumpy ☐ Noisy ☐ Friendly ☐ Ill ☐ Rebellious ☐ Energetic ☐

The activities I did today were...

[_____]

Today I learnt about...

[_____]

Today I have eaten...

Meal	What it was	All/most/some/none
Breakfast		
Snack		
Lunch		
Dessert		
Snack		
Dinner		
Dessert		

Please sign the medicine book ☐   Please provide some more:

Please sign the accident book ☐   _____

Today I slept...

Fell Asleep	Woke Up

Today my nappies were...

Time	Wet	Soiled	Dry	Checked

I had the following milk today...

Time	fl oz	Time	fl oz

Today I...

Went on the potty ☐   Went on the toilet ☐   I tried! ☐

Additional Notes...

Date (_____)

Today I have been...

Happy ☐ Chatty ☐ Quiet ☐ Sad ☐ Funny ☐ Tired ☐

Grumpy ☐ Noisy ☐ Friendly ☐ Ill ☐ Rebellious ☐ Energetic ☐

The activities I did today were...

Today I learnt about...

Today I have eaten...

Meal	What it was	All/most/some/none
Breakfast		
Snack		
Lunch		
Dessert		
Snack		
Dinner		
Dessert		

Please sign the medicine book ☐   Please provide some more:

Please sign the accident book ☐   _____

Today I slept...

Fell Asleep	Woke Up

Today my nappies were...

Time	Wet	Soiled	Dry	Checked

I had the following milk today...

Time	fl oz	Time	fl oz

Today I...

Went on the potty ☐ Went on the toilet ☐ I tried! ☐

Additional Notes...

Date ( )

Today I have been...

Happy ☐	Chatty ☐	Quiet ☐	Sad ☐	Funny ☐	Tired ☐
Grumpy ☐	Noisy ☐	Friendly ☐	Ill ☐	Rebellious ☐	Energetic ☐

The activities I did today were...

Today I learnt about...

Today I have eaten...

Meal	What it was	All/most/some/none
Breakfast		
Snack		
Lunch		
Dessert		
Snack		
Dinner		
Dessert		

Please sign the medicine book ☐ Please provide some more:

Please sign the accident book ☐ _____

Today I slept...

Fell Asleep	Woke Up

Today my nappies were...

Time	Wet	Soiled	Dry	Checked

I had the following milk today...

Time	fl oz	Time	fl oz

Today I...

Went on the potty ☐   Went on the toilet ☐   I tried! ☐

Additional Notes...

Observations

This weekend I...

Weekly Planning

	Trips	Activities	Notes
Monday			
Tuesday			
Wednesday			
Thursday			
Friday			

Parent's Notes

Monday

Tuesday

Wednesday

Thursday

Friday

Date _____

Today I have been...

| Happy ☐ | Chatty ☐ | Quiet ☐ | Sad ☐ | Funny ☐ | Tired ☐ |

| Grumpy ☐ | Noisy ☐ | Friendly ☐ | Ill ☐ | Rebellious ☐ | Energetic ☐ |

The activities I did today were...

Today I learnt about...

Today I have eaten...

Meal	What it was	All/most/some/none
Breakfast		
Snack		
Lunch		
Dessert		
Snack		
Dinner		
Dessert		

Please sign the medicine book ☐   Please provide some more:

Please sign the accident book ☐   _____

Today I slept...

Fell Asleep	Woke Up

Today my nappies were...

Time	Wet	Soiled	Dry	Checked

I had the following milk today...

Time	fl oz	Time	fl oz

Today I...

Went on the potty ☐   Went on the toilet ☐   I tried! ☐

Additional Notes...

Date [   ]

Today I have been...

Happy ☐ Chatty ☐ Quiet ☐ Sad ☐ Funny ☐ Tired ☐

Grumpy ☐ Noisy ☐ Friendly ☐ Ill ☐ Rebellious ☐ Energetic ☐

The activities I did today were...

[   ]

Today I learnt about...

[   ]

Today I have eaten...

Meal	What it was	All/most/some/none
Breakfast		
Snack		
Lunch		
Dessert		
Snack		
Dinner		
Dessert		

Please sign the medicine book ☐   Please provide some more:

Please sign the accident book ☐   _____

Today I slept...

Fell Asleep	Woke Up

Today my nappies were...

Time	Wet	Soiled	Dry	Checked

I had the following milk today...

Time	fl oz	Time	fl oz

Today I...

Went on the potty ☐   Went on the toilet ☐   I tried! ☐

Additional Notes...

Date

Today I have been...

Happy ☐	Chatty ☐	Quiet ☐	Sad ☐	Funny ☐	Tired ☐
Grumpy ☐	Noisy ☐	Friendly ☐	Ill ☐	Rebellious ☐	Energetic ☐

The activities I did today were...

Today I learnt about...

Today I have eaten...

Meal	What it was	All/most/some/none
Breakfast		
Snack		
Lunch		
Dessert		
Snack		
Dinner		
Dessert		

Please sign the medicine book ☐   Please provide some more:

Please sign the accident book ☐   _____

Today I slept...

Fell Asleep	Woke Up

Today my nappies were...

Time	Wet	Soiled	Dry	Checked

I had the following milk today...

Time	fl oz	Time	fl oz

Today I...

Went on the potty ☐   Went on the toilet ☐   I tried! ☐

Additional Notes...

Date (   )

Today I have been...

Happy ☐	Chatty ☐	Quiet ☐	Sad ☐	Funny ☐	Tired ☐
Grumpy ☐	Noisy ☐	Friendly ☐	Ill ☐	Rebellious ☐	Energetic ☐

The activities I did today were...

Today I learnt about...

Today I have eaten...

Meal	What it was	All/most/some/none
Breakfast		
Snack		
Lunch		
Dessert		
Snack		
Dinner		
Dessert		

Please sign the medicine book ☐   Please provide some more:

Please sign the accident book ☐   _____

Today I slept...

Fell Asleep	Woke Up

Today my nappies were...

Time	Wet	Soiled	Dry	Checked

I had the following milk today...

Time	fl oz	Time	fl oz

Today I...

Went on the potty ☐ Went on the toilet ☐ I tried! ☐

Additional Notes...

Date [   ]

Today I have been...

Happy ☐	Chatty ☐	Quiet ☐	Sad ☐	Funny ☐	Tired ☐
Grumpy ☐	Noisy ☐	Friendly ☐	Ill ☐	Rebellious ☐	Energetic ☐

The activities I did today were...

[   ]

Today I learnt about...

[   ]

Today I have eaten...

Meal	What it was	All/most/some/none
Breakfast		
Snack		
Lunch		
Dessert		
Snack		
Dinner		
Dessert		

Please sign the medicine book ☐   Please provide some more:

Please sign the accident book ☐   _____

Today I slept...

Fell Asleep	Woke Up

Today my nappies were...

Time	Wet	Soiled	Dry	Checked

I had the following milk today...

Time	fl oz	Time	fl oz

Today I...

Went on the potty ☐   Went on the toilet ☐   I tried! ☐

Additional Notes...

Observations

This weekend I...

Weekly Planning

	Trips	Activities	Notes
Monday			
Tuesday			
Wednesday			
Thursday			
Friday			

Parent's Notes

Monday
Tuesday
Wednesday
Thursday
Friday

Date [   ]

Today I have been...

Happy ☐   Chatty ☐   Quiet ☐   Sad ☐   Funny ☐   Tired ☐

Grumpy ☐   Noisy ☐   Friendly ☐   Ill ☐   Rebellious ☐   Energetic ☐

The activities I did today were...

[   ]

Today I learnt about...

[   ]

Today I have eaten...

Meal	What it was	All/most/some/none
Breakfast		
Snack		
Lunch		
Dessert		
Snack		
Dinner		
Dessert		

Please sign the medicine book ☐   Please provide some more:

Please sign the accident book ☐   _____

Today I slept...

Fell Asleep	Woke Up

Today my nappies were...

Time	Wet	Soiled	Dry	Checked

I had the following milk today...

Time	fl oz	Time	fl oz

Today I...

Went on the potty ☐   Went on the toilet ☐   I tried! ☐

Additional Notes...

Date

Today I have been...

Happy ☐ Chatty ☐ Quiet ☐ Sad ☐ Funny ☐ Tired ☐

Grumpy ☐ Noisy ☐ Friendly ☐ Ill ☐ Rebellious ☐ Energetic ☐

The activities I did today were...

Today I learnt about...

Today I have eaten...

Meal	What it was	All/most/some/none
Breakfast		
Snack		
Lunch		
Dessert		
Snack		
Dinner		
Dessert		

Please sign the medicine book ☐   Please provide some more:

Please sign the accident book ☐   _____

Today I slept...

Fell Asleep	Woke Up

Today my nappies were...

Time	Wet	Soiled	Dry	Checked

I had the following milk today...

Time	fl oz	Time	fl oz

Today I...

Went on the potty ☐   Went on the toilet ☐   I tried! ☐

Additional Notes...

Date [   ]

Today I have been...

Happy ☐	Chatty ☐	Quiet ☐	Sad ☐	Funny ☐	Tired ☐
Grumpy ☐	Noisy ☐	Friendly ☐	Ill ☐	Rebellious ☐	Energetic ☐

The activities I did today were...

[   ]

Today I learnt about...

[   ]

Today I have eaten...

Meal	What it was	All/most/some/none
Breakfast		
Snack		
Lunch		
Dessert		
Snack		
Dinner		
Dessert		

Please sign the medicine book ☐   Please provide some more:

Please sign the accident book ☐   _____

Today I slept...

Fell Asleep	Woke Up

Today my nappies were...

Time	Wet	Soiled	Dry	Checked

I had the following milk today...

Time	fl oz	Time	fl oz

Today I...

Went on the potty ☐ Went on the toilet ☐ I tried! ☐

Additional Notes...

Date

Today I have been...

Happy ☐ Chatty ☐ Quiet ☐ Sad ☐ Funny ☐ Tired ☐

Grumpy ☐ Noisy ☐ Friendly ☐ Ill ☐ Rebellious ☐ Energetic ☐

The activities I did today were...

Today I learnt about...

Today I have eaten...

Meal	What it was	All/most/some/none
Breakfast		
Snack		
Lunch		
Dessert		
Snack		
Dinner		
Dessert		

Please sign the medicine book ☐   Please provide some more:

Please sign the accident book ☐   _____

Today I slept...

Fell Asleep	Woke Up

Today my nappies were...

Time	Wet	Soiled	Dry	Checked

I had the following milk today...

Time	fl oz	Time	fl oz

Today I...

Went on the potty ☐   Went on the toilet ☐   I tried! ☐

Additional Notes...

Date

Today I have been...

Happy ☐ Chatty ☐ Quiet ☐ Sad ☐ Funny ☐ Tired ☐

Grumpy ☐ Noisy ☐ Friendly ☐ Ill ☐ Rebellious ☐ Energetic ☐

The activities I did today were...

Today I learnt about...

Today I have eaten...

Meal	What it was	All/most/some/none
Breakfast		
Snack		
Lunch		
Dessert		
Snack		
Dinner		
Dessert		

Please sign the medicine book ☐   Please provide some more:

Please sign the accident book ☐   _____

Today I slept...

Fell Asleep	Woke Up

Today my nappies were...

Time	Wet	Soiled	Dry	Checked

I had the following milk today...

Time	fl oz	Time	fl oz

Today I...

Went on the potty ☐   Went on the toilet ☐   I tried! ☐

Additional Notes...

Observations

This weekend I...

This weekend I...

Weekly Planning

	Trips	Activities	Notes
Monday			
Tuesday			
Wednesday			
Thursday			
Friday			

Parent's Notes

Monday

Tuesday

Wednesday

Thursday

Friday

Date

Today I have been...

| Happy ☐ | Chatty ☐ | Quiet ☐ | Sad ☐ | Funny ☐ | Tired ☐ |
| Grumpy ☐ | Noisy ☐ | Friendly ☐ | Ill ☐ | Rebellious ☐ | Energetic ☐ |

The activities I did today were...

Today I learnt about...

Today I have eaten...

Meal	What it was	All/most/some/none
Breakfast		
Snack		
Lunch		
Dessert		
Snack		
Dinner		
Dessert		

Please sign the medicine book ☐   Please provide some more:

Please sign the accident book ☐   _____

Today I slept...

Fell Asleep	Woke Up

Today my nappies were...

Time	Wet	Soiled	Dry	Checked

I had the following milk today...

Time	fl oz	Time	fl oz

Today I...

Went on the potty ☐   Went on the toilet ☐   I tried! ☐

Additional Notes...

Date [_____]

Today I have been...

Happy ☐ Chatty ☐ Quiet ☐ Sad ☐ Funny ☐ Tired ☐

Grumpy ☐ Noisy ☐ Friendly ☐ Ill ☐ Rebellious ☐ Energetic ☐

The activities I did today were...

[_____]

Today I learnt about...

[_____]

Today I have eaten...

Meal	What it was	All/most/some/none
Breakfast		
Snack		
Lunch		
Dessert		
Snack		
Dinner		
Dessert		

Please sign the medicine book ☐   Please provide some more:

Please sign the accident book ☐   _____

Today I slept...

Fell Asleep	Woke Up

Today my nappies were...

Time	Wet	Soiled	Dry	Checked

I had the following milk today...

Time	fl oz	Time	fl oz

Today I...

Went on the potty ☐   Went on the toilet ☐   I tried! ☐

Additional Notes...

Date _____

Today I have been...

Happy ☐   Chatty ☐   Quiet ☐   Sad ☐   Funny ☐   Tired ☐

Grumpy ☐   Noisy ☐   Friendly ☐   Ill ☐   Rebellious ☐   Energetic ☐

The activities I did today were...

Today I learnt about...

Today I have eaten...

Meal	What it was	All/most/some/none
Breakfast		
Snack		
Lunch		
Dessert		
Snack		
Dinner		
Dessert		

Please sign the medicine book ☐   Please provide some more:

Please sign the accident book ☐   _____

Today I slept...

Fell Asleep	Woke Up

Today my nappies were...

Time	Wet	Soiled	Dry	Checked

I had the following milk today...

Time	fl oz	Time	fl oz

Today I...

Went on the potty ☐   Went on the toilet ☐   I tried! ☐

Additional Notes...

Date (   )

Today I have been...

Happy ☐   Chatty ☐   Quiet ☐   Sad ☐   Funny ☐   Tired ☐

Grumpy ☐   Noisy ☐   Friendly ☐   Ill ☐   Rebellious ☐   Energetic ☐

The activities I did today were...

Today I learnt about...

Today I have eaten...

Meal	What it was	All/most/some/none
Breakfast		
Snack		
Lunch		
Dessert		
Snack		
Dinner		
Dessert		

Please sign the medicine book ☐   Please provide some more:

Please sign the accident book ☐   _____

Today I slept...

Fell Asleep	Woke Up

Today my nappies were...

Time	Wet	Soiled	Dry	Checked

I had the following milk today...

Time	fl oz	Time	fl oz

Today I...

Went on the potty ☐　Went on the toilet ☐　I tried! ☐

Additional Notes...

Date [   ]

Today I have been...

Happy ☐　Chatty ☐　Quiet ☐　Sad ☐　Funny ☐　Tired ☐

Grumpy ☐　Noisy ☐　Friendly ☐　Ill ☐　Rebellious ☐　Energetic ☐

The activities I did today were...

[   ]

Today I learnt about...

[   ]

Today I have eaten...

Meal	What it was	All/most/some/none
Breakfast		
Snack		
Lunch		
Dessert		
Snack		
Dinner		
Dessert		

Please sign the medicine book ☐　Please provide some more:

Please sign the accident book ☐　_____

Today I slept...

Fell Asleep	Woke Up

Today my nappies were...

Time	Wet	Soiled	Dry	Checked

I had the following milk today...

Time	fl oz	Time	fl oz

Today I...

Went on the potty ☐ Went on the toilet ☐ I tried! ☐

Additional Notes...

Observations

This weekend I...

Weekly Planning

	Trips	Activities	Notes
Monday			
Tuesday			
Wednesday			
Thursday			
Friday			

Parent's Notes

Monday

Tuesday

Wednesday

Thursday

Friday

Date

Today I have been...

Happy ☐ Chatty ☐ Quiet ☐ Sad ☐ Funny☐ Tired ☐

Grumpy ☐ Noisy ☐ Friendly ☐ Ill ☐ Rebellious☐ Energetic☐

The activities I did today were...

Today I learnt about...

Today I have eaten...

Meal	What it was	All/most/some/none
Breakfast		
Snack		
Lunch		
Dessert		
Snack		
Dinner		
Dessert		

Please sign the medicine book ☐ Please provide some more:

Please sign the accident book ☐ _____

Today I slept...

Fell Asleep	Woke Up

Today my nappies were...

Time	Wet	Soiled	Dry	Checked

I had the following milk today...

Time	fl oz	Time	fl oz

Today I...

Went on the potty ☐   Went on the toilet ☐   I tried! ☐

Additional Notes...

Date

Today I have been...

Happy ☐   Chatty ☐   Quiet ☐   Sad ☐   Funny ☐   Tired ☐

Grumpy ☐   Noisy ☐   Friendly ☐   Ill ☐   Rebellious ☐   Energetic ☐

The activities I did today were...

Today I learnt about...

Today I have eaten...

Meal	What it was	All/most/some/none
Breakfast		
Snack		
Lunch		
Dessert		
Snack		
Dinner		
Dessert		

Please sign the medicine book ☐   Please provide some more:

Please sign the accident book ☐   _____

Today I slept...

Fell Asleep	Woke Up

Today my nappies were...

Time	Wet	Soiled	Dry	Checked

I had the following milk today...

Time	fl oz	Time	fl oz

Today I...

Went on the potty ☐   Went on the toilet ☐   I tried! ☐

Additional Notes...

Date ⬭

Today I have been...

| Happy ☐ | Chatty ☐ | Quiet ☐ | Sad ☐ | Funny ☐ | Tired ☐ |

| Grumpy ☐ | Noisy ☐ | Friendly ☐ | Ill ☐ | Rebellious ☐ | Energetic ☐ |

The activities I did today were...

Today I learnt about...

Today I have eaten...

Meal	What it was	All/most/some/none
Breakfast		
Snack		
Lunch		
Dessert		
Snack		
Dinner		
Dessert		

Please sign the medicine book ☐   Please provide some more:

Please sign the accident book ☐   _____

Today I slept...

Fell Asleep	Woke Up

Today my nappies were...

Time	Wet	Soiled	Dry	Checked

I had the following milk today...

Time	fl oz	Time	fl oz

Today I...

 Went on the potty ☐   Went on the toilet ☐   I tried! ☐

Additional Notes...

Date [_____]

Today I have been...

Happy ☐   Chatty ☐   Quiet ☐   Sad ☐   Funny ☐   Tired ☐

Grumpy ☐   Noisy ☐   Friendly ☐   Ill ☐   Rebellious ☐   Energetic ☐

The activities I did today were...

[_____]

Today I learnt about...

[_____]

Today I have eaten...

Meal	What it was	All/most/some/none
Breakfast		
Snack		
Lunch		
Dessert		
Snack		
Dinner		
Dessert		

Please sign the medicine book ☐   Please provide some more:

Please sign the accident book ☐   _____

Today I slept...

Fell Asleep	Woke Up

Today my nappies were...

Time	Wet	Soiled	Dry	Checked

I had the following milk today...

Time	fl oz	Time	fl oz

Today I...

Went on the potty ☐ Went on the toilet ☐ I tried! ☐

Additional Notes...

Date ⬭

Today I have been...

Happy ☐ Chatty ☐ Quiet ☐ Sad ☐ Funny ☐ Tired ☐

Grumpy ☐ Noisy ☐ Friendly ☐ Ill ☐ Rebellious ☐ Energetic ☐

The activities I did today were...

Today I learnt about...

Today I have eaten...

Meal	What it was	All/most/some/none
Breakfast		
Snack		
Lunch		
Dessert		
Snack		
Dinner		
Dessert		

Please sign the medicine book ☐   Please provide some more:

Please sign the accident book ☐   _____

Today I slept...

Fell Asleep	Woke Up

Today my nappies were...

Time	Wet	Soiled	Dry	Checked

I had the following milk today...

Time	fl oz	Time	fl oz

Today I...

Went on the potty ☐   Went on the toilet ☐   I tried! ☐

Additional Notes...

Observations

This weekend I...

Weekly Planning

	Trips	Activities	Notes
Monday			
Tuesday			
Wednesday			
Thursday			
Friday			

Parent's Notes

Monday

Tuesday

Wednesday

Thursday

Friday

Date

Today I have been...

Happy ☐ Chatty ☐ Quiet ☐ Sad ☐ Funny ☐ Tired ☐

Grumpy ☐ Noisy ☐ Friendly ☐ Ill ☐ Rebellious ☐ Energetic ☐

The activities I did today were...

Today I learnt about...

Today I have eaten...

Meal	What it was	All/most/some/none
Breakfast		
Snack		
Lunch		
Dessert		
Snack		
Dinner		
Dessert		

Please sign the medicine book ☐   Please provide some more:

Please sign the accident book ☐   _____

Today I slept...

Fell Asleep	Woke Up

Today my nappies were...

Time	Wet	Soiled	Dry	Checked

I had the following milk today...

Time	fl oz	Time	fl oz

Today I...

Went on the potty ☐ Went on the toilet ☐ I tried! ☐

Additional Notes...

Date ⬭

Today I have been...

Happy ☐ Chatty ☐ Quiet ☐ Sad ☐ Funny ☐ Tired ☐

Grumpy ☐ Noisy ☐ Friendly ☐ Ill ☐ Rebellious ☐ Energetic ☐

The activities I did today were...

Today I learnt about...

Today I have eaten...

Meal	What it was	All/most/some/none
Breakfast		
Snack		
Lunch		
Dessert		
Snack		
Dinner		
Dessert		

Please sign the medicine book ☐   Please provide some more:

Please sign the accident book ☐   _____

Today I slept...

Fell Asleep	Woke Up

Today my nappies were...

Time	Wet	Soiled	Dry	Checked

I had the following milk today...

Time	fl oz	Time	fl oz

Today I...

Went on the potty ☐   Went on the toilet ☐   I tried! ☐

Additional Notes...

Date

Today I have been...

Happy ☐   Chatty ☐   Quiet ☐   Sad ☐   Funny ☐   Tired ☐

Grumpy ☐   Noisy ☐   Friendly ☐   Ill ☐   Rebellious ☐   Energetic ☐

The activities I did today were...

Today I learnt about...

Today I have eaten...

Meal	What it was	All/most/some/none
Breakfast		
Snack		
Lunch		
Dessert		
Snack		
Dinner		
Dessert		

Please sign the medicine book ☐   Please provide some more:

Please sign the accident book ☐   _____

Today I slept...

Fell Asleep	Woke Up

Today my nappies were...

Time	Wet	Soiled	Dry	Checked

I had the following milk today...

Time	fl oz	Time	fl oz

Today I...

Went on the potty ☐   Went on the toilet ☐   I tried! ☐

Additional Notes...

Date

Today I have been...

Happy ☐	Chatty ☐	Quiet ☐	Sad ☐	Funny ☐	Tired ☐
Grumpy ☐	Noisy ☐	Friendly ☐	Ill ☐	Rebellious ☐	Energetic ☐

The activities I did today were...

Today I learnt about...

Today I have eaten...

Meal	What it was	All/most/some/none
Breakfast		
Snack		
Lunch		
Dessert		
Snack		
Dinner		
Dessert		

Please sign the medicine book ☐   Please provide some more:

Please sign the accident book ☐   _____

Today I slept...

Fell Asleep	Woke Up

Today my nappies were...

Time	Wet	Soiled	Dry	Checked

I had the following milk today...

Time	fl oz	Time	fl oz

Today I...

Went on the potty ☐   Went on the toilet ☐   I tried! ☐

Additional Notes...

Date (_____)

Today I have been...

Happy ☐ Chatty ☐ Quiet ☐ Sad ☐ Funny ☐ Tired ☐

Grumpy ☐ Noisy ☐ Friendly ☐ Ill ☐ Rebellious ☐ Energetic ☐

The activities I did today were...

Today I learnt about...

Today I have eaten...

Meal	What it was	All/most/some/none
Breakfast		
Snack		
Lunch		
Dessert		
Snack		
Dinner		
Dessert		

Please sign the medicine book ☐   Please provide some more:

Please sign the accident book ☐   _____

Today I slept...

Fell Asleep	Woke Up

Today my nappies were...

Time	Wet	Soiled	Dry	Checked

I had the following milk today...

Time	fl oz	Time	fl oz

Today I...

Went on the potty ☐   Went on the toilet ☐   I tried! ☐

Additional Notes...

Observations

This weekend I...

This weekend I...

Weekly Planning

	Trips	Activities	Notes
Monday			
Tuesday			
Wednesday			
Thursday			
Friday			

Parent's Notes

Monday
Tuesday
Wednesday
Thursday
Friday

Date ( )

Today I have been...

Happy ☐ Chatty ☐ Quiet ☐ Sad ☐ Funny ☐ Tired ☐

Grumpy ☐ Noisy ☐ Friendly ☐ Ill ☐ Rebellious ☐ Energetic ☐

The activities I did today were...

Today I learnt about...

Today I have eaten...

Meal	What it was	All/most/some/none
Breakfast		
Snack		
Lunch		
Dessert		
Snack		
Dinner		
Dessert		

Please sign the medicine book ☐   Please provide some more:

Please sign the accident book ☐   _____

Today I slept...

Fell Asleep	Woke Up

Today my nappies were...

Time	Wet	Soiled	Dry	Checked

I had the following milk today...

Time	fl oz	Time	fl oz

Today I...

Went on the potty ☐ Went on the toilet ☐ I tried! ☐

Additional Notes...

Date ( )

Today I have been...

Happy ☐ Chatty ☐ Quiet ☐ Sad ☐ Funny ☐ Tired ☐

Grumpy ☐ Noisy ☐ Friendly ☐ Ill ☐ Rebellious ☐ Energetic ☐

The activities I did today were...

( )

Today I learnt about...

( )

Today I have eaten...

Meal	What it was	All/most/some/none
Breakfast		
Snack		
Lunch		
Dessert		
Snack		
Dinner		
Dessert		

Please sign the medicine book ☐ Please provide some more:

Please sign the accident book ☐ _____

Today I slept...

Fell Asleep	Woke Up

Today my nappies were...

Time	Wet	Soiled	Dry	Checked

I had the following milk today...

Time	fl oz	Time	fl oz

Today I...

Went on the potty ☐   Went on the toilet ☐   I tried! ☐

Additional Notes...

Date ⬭

Today I have been...

Happy ☐   Chatty ☐   Quiet ☐   Sad ☐   Funny ☐   Tired ☐

Grumpy ☐   Noisy ☐   Friendly ☐   Ill ☐   Rebellious ☐   Energetic ☐

The activities I did today were...

Today I learnt about...

Today I have eaten...

Meal	What it was	All/most/some/none
Breakfast		
Snack		
Lunch		
Dessert		
Snack		
Dinner		
Dessert		

Please sign the medicine book ☐   Please provide some more:

Please sign the accident book ☐   _____

Today I slept...

Fell Asleep	Woke Up

Today my nappies were...

Time	Wet	Soiled	Dry	Checked

I had the following milk today...

Time	fl oz	Time	fl oz

Today I...

Went on the potty ☐   Went on the toilet ☐   I tried! ☐

Additional Notes...

Date _____

Today I have been...

| Happy ☐ | Chatty ☐ | Quiet ☐ | Sad ☐ | Funny ☐ | Tired ☐ |

| Grumpy ☐ | Noisy ☐ | Friendly ☐ | Ill ☐ | Rebellious ☐ | Energetic ☐ |

The activities I did today were...

Today I learnt about...

Today I have eaten...

Meal	What it was	All/most/some/none
Breakfast		
Snack		
Lunch		
Dessert		
Snack		
Dinner		
Dessert		

Please sign the medicine book ☐   Please provide some more:

Please sign the accident book ☐   _____

Today I slept...

Fell Asleep	Woke Up

Today my nappies were...

Time	Wet	Soiled	Dry	Checked

I had the following milk today...

Time	fl oz	Time	fl oz

Today I...

Went on the potty ☐ Went on the toilet ☐   I tried! ☐

Additional Notes...

Date

Today I have been...

Happy ☐ Chatty ☐ Quiet ☐ Sad ☐ Funny ☐ Tired ☐

Grumpy ☐ Noisy ☐ Friendly ☐ Ill ☐ Rebellious ☐ Energetic ☐

The activities I did today were...

Today I learnt about...

Today I have eaten...

Meal	What it was	All/most/some/none
Breakfast		
Snack		
Lunch		
Dessert		
Snack		
Dinner		
Dessert		

Please sign the medicine book ☐   Please provide some more:

Please sign the accident book ☐   _____

Today I slept...

Fell Asleep	Woke Up

Today my nappies were...

Time	Wet	Soiled	Dry	Checked

I had the following milk today...

Time	fl oz	Time	fl oz

Today I...

Went on the potty ☐ Went on the toilet ☐ I tried! ☐

Additional Notes...

Observations

This weekend I...

Weekly Planning

	Trips	Activities	Notes
Monday			
Tuesday			
Wednesday			
Thursday			
Friday			

Parent's Notes

Monday

Tuesday

Wednesday

Thursday

Friday

Date ⬭

Today I have been...

Happy ☐ Chatty ☐ Quiet ☐ Sad ☐ Funny ☐ Tired ☐

Grumpy ☐ Noisy ☐ Friendly ☐ Ill ☐ Rebellious ☐ Energetic ☐

The activities I did today were...

Today I learnt about...

Today I have eaten...

Meal	What it was	All/most/some/none
Breakfast		
Snack		
Lunch		
Dessert		
Snack		
Dinner		
Dessert		

Please sign the medicine book ☐ Please provide some more:

Please sign the accident book ☐ _____

Today I slept...

Fell Asleep	Woke Up

Today my nappies were...

Time	Wet	Soiled	Dry	Checked

I had the following milk today...

Time	fl oz	Time	fl oz

Today I...

Went on the potty ☐   Went on the toilet ☐   I tried! ☐

Additional Notes...

Date [_____]

Today I have been...

Happy ☐	Chatty ☐	Quiet ☐	Sad ☐	Funny ☐	Tired ☐
Grumpy ☐	Noisy ☐	Friendly ☐	Ill ☐	Rebellious ☐	Energetic ☐

The activities I did today were...

[_____]

Today I learnt about...

[_____]

Today I have eaten...

Meal	What it was	All/most/some/none
Breakfast		
Snack		
Lunch		
Dessert		
Snack		
Dinner		
Dessert		

Please sign the medicine book ☐   Please provide some more:

Please sign the accident book ☐   _____

Today I slept...

Fell Asleep	Woke Up

Today my nappies were...

Time	Wet	Soiled	Dry	Checked

I had the following milk today...

Time	fl oz	Time	fl oz

Today I...

Went on the potty ☐   Went on the toilet ☐   I tried! ☐

Additional Notes...

Date

Today I have been...

| Happy ☐ | Chatty ☐ | Quiet ☐ | Sad ☐ | Funny ☐ | Tired ☐ |

| Grumpy ☐ | Noisy ☐ | Friendly ☐ | Ill ☐ | Rebellious ☐ | Energetic ☐ |

The activities I did today were...

Today I learnt about...

Today I have eaten...

Meal	What it was	All/most/some/none
Breakfast		
Snack		
Lunch		
Dessert		
Snack		
Dinner		
Dessert		

Please sign the medicine book ☐   Please provide some more:

Please sign the accident book ☐   _____

Today I slept...

Fell Asleep	Woke Up

Today my nappies were...

Time	Wet	Soiled	Dry	Checked

I had the following milk today...

Time	fl oz	Time	fl oz

Today I...

Went on the potty ☐   Went on the toilet ☐   I tried! ☐

Additional Notes...

Date (_____)

Today I have been...

Happy ☐ Chatty ☐ Quiet ☐ Sad ☐ Funny ☐ Tired ☐

Grumpy ☐ Noisy ☐ Friendly ☐ Ill ☐ Rebellious ☐ Energetic ☐

The activities I did today were...

Today I learnt about...

Today I have eaten...

Meal	What it was	All/most/some/none
Breakfast		
Snack		
Lunch		
Dessert		
Snack		
Dinner		
Dessert		

Please sign the medicine book ☐   Please provide some more:

Please sign the accident book ☐   _____

Today I slept...

Fell Asleep	Woke Up

Today my nappies were...

Time	Wet	Soiled	Dry	Checked

I had the following milk today...

Time	fl oz	Time	fl oz

Today I...

Went on the potty ☐   Went on the toilet ☐   I tried! ☐

Additional Notes...

Date (   )

Today I have been...

Happy ☐	Chatty ☐	Quiet ☐	Sad ☐	Funny ☐	Tired ☐
Grumpy ☐	Noisy ☐	Friendly ☐	Ill ☐	Rebellious ☐	Energetic ☐

The activities I did today were...

Today I learnt about...

Today I have eaten...

Meal	What it was	All/most/some/none
Breakfast		
Snack		
Lunch		
Dessert		
Snack		
Dinner		
Dessert		

Please sign the medicine book ☐   Please provide some more:

Please sign the accident book ☐   _____

Today I slept...

Fell Asleep	Woke Up

Today my nappies were...

Time	Wet	Soiled	Dry	Checked

I had the following milk today...

Time	fl oz	Time	fl oz

Today I...

Went on the potty ☐   Went on the toilet ☐   I tried! ☐

Additional Notes...

Observations

This weekend I...

Weekly Planning

	Trips	Activities	Notes
Monday			
Tuesday			
Wednesday			
Thursday			
Friday			

Parent's Notes

Monday

Tuesday

Wednesday

Thursday

Friday

Date [   ]

Today I have been...

Happy ☐	Chatty ☐	Quiet ☐	Sad ☐	Funny ☐	Tired ☐
Grumpy ☐	Noisy ☐	Friendly ☐	Ill ☐	Rebellious ☐	Energetic ☐

The activities I did today were...

[   ]

Today I learnt about...

[   ]

Today I have eaten...

Meal	What it was	All/most/some/none
Breakfast		
Snack		
Lunch		
Dessert		
Snack		
Dinner		
Dessert		

Please sign the medicine book ☐   Please provide some more:

Please sign the accident book ☐   _____

Today I slept...

Fell Asleep	Woke Up

Today my nappies were...

Time	Wet	Soiled	Dry	Checked

I had the following milk today...

Time	fl oz	Time	fl oz

Today I...

Went on the potty ☐ Went on the toilet ☐ I tried! ☐

Additional Notes...

Date

Today I have been...

Happy ☐	Chatty ☐	Quiet ☐	Sad ☐	Funny ☐	Tired ☐
Grumpy ☐	Noisy ☐	Friendly ☐	Ill ☐	Rebellious ☐	Energetic ☐

The activities I did today were...

Today I learnt about...

Today I have eaten...

Meal	What it was	All/most/some/none
Breakfast		
Snack		
Lunch		
Dessert		
Snack		
Dinner		
Dessert		

Please sign the medicine book ☐   Please provide some more:

Please sign the accident book ☐   _____

Today I slept...

Fell Asleep	Woke Up

Today my nappies were...

Time	Wet	Soiled	Dry	Checked

I had the following milk today...

Time	fl oz	Time	fl oz

Today I...

Went on the potty ☐   Went on the toilet ☐   I tried! ☐

Additional Notes...

Date ⬭

Today I have been...

Happy ☐ Chatty ☐ Quiet ☐ Sad ☐ Funny ☐ Tired ☐

Grumpy ☐ Noisy ☐ Friendly ☐ Ill ☐ Rebellious ☐ Energetic ☐

The activities I did today were...

⬭

Today I learnt about...

⬭

Today I have eaten...

Meal	What it was	All/most/some/none
Breakfast		
Snack		
Lunch		
Dessert		
Snack		
Dinner		
Dessert		

Please sign the medicine book ☐   Please provide some more:

Please sign the accident book ☐   _____

Today I slept...

Fell Asleep	Woke Up

Today my nappies were...

Time	Wet	Soiled	Dry	Checked

I had the following milk today...

Time	fl oz	Time	fl oz

Today I...

Went on the potty ☐   Went on the toilet ☐   I tried! ☐

Additional Notes...

Date ( )

Today I have been...

Happy ☐	Chatty ☐	Quiet ☐	Sad ☐	Funny ☐	Tired ☐

Grumpy ☐	Noisy ☐	Friendly ☐	Ill ☐	Rebellious ☐	Energetic ☐

The activities I did today were...

Today I learnt about...

Today I have eaten...

Meal	What it was	All/most/some/none
Breakfast		
Snack		
Lunch		
Dessert		
Snack		
Dinner		
Dessert		

Please sign the medicine book ☐   Please provide some more:

Please sign the accident book ☐   _____

Today I slept...

Fell Asleep	Woke Up

Today my nappies were...

Time	Wet	Soiled	Dry	Checked

I had the following milk today...

Time	fl oz	Time	fl oz

Today I...

Went on the potty ☐   Went on the toilet ☐   I tried! ☐

Additional Notes...

Date ⬭

Today I have been...

Happy ☐ Chatty ☐ Quiet ☐ Sad ☐ Funny ☐ Tired ☐

Grumpy ☐ Noisy ☐ Friendly ☐ Ill ☐ Rebellious ☐ Energetic ☐

The activities I did today were...

Today I learnt about...

Today I have eaten...

Meal	What it was	All/most/some/none
Breakfast		
Snack		
Lunch		
Dessert		
Snack		
Dinner		
Dessert		

Please sign the medicine book ☐   Please provide some more:

Please sign the accident book ☐   _____

Today I slept...

Fell Asleep	Woke Up

Today my nappies were...

Time	Wet	Soiled	Dry	Checked

I had the following milk today...

Time	fl oz	Time	fl oz

Today I...

Went on the potty ☐ Went on the toilet ☐ I tried! ☐

Additional Notes...

Observations

This weekend I...

Weekly Planning

	Trips	Activities	Notes
Monday			
Tuesday			
Wednesday			
Thursday			
Friday			

Parent's Notes

Monday

Tuesday

Wednesday

Thursday

Friday

Date _____

Today I have been...

Happy ☐ Chatty ☐ Quiet ☐ Sad ☐ Funny ☐ Tired ☐

Grumpy ☐ Noisy ☐ Friendly ☐ Ill ☐ Rebellious ☐ Energetic ☐

The activities I did today were...

_____

Today I learnt about...

_____

Today I have eaten...

Meal	What it was	All/most/some/none
Breakfast		
Snack		
Lunch		
Dessert		
Snack		
Dinner		
Dessert		

Please sign the medicine book ☐   Please provide some more:

Please sign the accident book ☐   _____

Today I slept...

Fell Asleep	Woke Up

Today my nappies were...

Time	Wet	Soiled	Dry	Checked

I had the following milk today...

Time	fl oz	Time	fl oz

Today I...

Went on the potty ☐ Went on the toilet ☐ I tried! ☐

Additional Notes...

Date ⬭

Today I have been...

Happy ☐ Chatty ☐ Quiet ☐ Sad ☐ Funny ☐ Tired ☐

Grumpy ☐ Noisy ☐ Friendly ☐ Ill ☐ Rebellious ☐ Energetic ☐

The activities I did today were...

Today I learnt about...

Today I have eaten...

Meal	What it was	All/most/some/none
Breakfast		
Snack		
Lunch		
Dessert		
Snack		
Dinner		
Dessert		

Please sign the medicine book ☐   Please provide some more:

Please sign the accident book ☐   _____

Today I slept...

Fell Asleep	Woke Up

Today my nappies were...

Time	Wet	Soiled	Dry	Checked

I had the following milk today...

Time	fl oz	Time	fl oz

Today I...

Went on the potty ☐   Went on the toilet ☐   I tried! ☐

Additional Notes...

Date

Today I have been...

Happy ☐ Chatty ☐ Quiet ☐ Sad ☐ Funny ☐ Tired ☐

Grumpy ☐ Noisy ☐ Friendly ☐ Ill ☐ Rebellious ☐ Energetic ☐

The activities I did today were...

Today I learnt about...

Today I have eaten...

Meal	What it was	All/most/some/none
Breakfast		
Snack		
Lunch		
Dessert		
Snack		
Dinner		
Dessert		

Please sign the medicine book ☐   Please provide some more:

Please sign the accident book ☐   _____

Today I slept...

Fell Asleep	Woke Up

Today my nappies were...

Time	Wet	Soiled	Dry	Checked

I had the following milk today...

Time	fl oz	Time	fl oz

Today I...

Went on the potty ☐   Went on the toilet ☐   I tried! ☐

Additional Notes...

Date (_____)

Today I have been...

Happy ☐	Chatty ☐	Quiet ☐	Sad ☐	Funny ☐	Tired ☐
Grumpy ☐	Noisy ☐	Friendly ☐	Ill ☐	Rebellious ☐	Energetic ☐

The activities I did today were...

[ ]

Today I learnt about...

[ ]

Today I have eaten...

Meal	What it was	All/most/some/none
Breakfast		
Snack		
Lunch		
Dessert		
Snack		
Dinner		
Dessert		

Please sign the medicine book ☐   Please provide some more:

Please sign the accident book ☐   _____

Today I slept...

Fell Asleep	Woke Up

Today my nappies were...

Time	Wet	Soiled	Dry	Checked

I had the following milk today...

Time	fl oz	Time	fl oz

Today I...

Went on the potty ☐   Went on the toilet ☐   I tried! ☐

Additional Notes...

Date

Today I have been...

Happy ☐	Chatty ☐	Quiet ☐	Sad ☐	Funny ☐	Tired ☐
Grumpy ☐	Noisy ☐	Friendly ☐	Ill ☐	Rebellious ☐	Energetic ☐

The activities I did today were...

Today I learnt about...

Today I have eaten...

Meal	What it was	All/most/some/none
Breakfast		
Snack		
Lunch		
Dessert		
Snack		
Dinner		
Dessert		

Please sign the medicine book ☐   Please provide some more:

Please sign the accident book ☐   _____

Today I slept...

Fell Asleep	Woke Up

Today my nappies were...

Time	Wet	Soiled	Dry	Checked

I had the following milk today...

Time	fl oz	Time	fl oz

Today I...

Went on the potty ☐   Went on the toilet ☐   I tried! ☐

Additional Notes...

Observations

This weekend I...

Weekly Planning

	Trips	Activities	Notes
Monday			
Tuesday			
Wednesday			
Thursday			
Friday			

Parent's Notes

Monday

Tuesday

Wednesday

Thursday

Friday

Date (⬚)

Today I have been...

Happy ☐ Chatty ☐ Quiet ☐ Sad ☐ Funny ☐ Tired ☐

Grumpy ☐ Noisy ☐ Friendly ☐ Ill ☐ Rebellious ☐ Energetic ☐

The activities I did today were...

Today I learnt about...

Today I have eaten...

Meal	What it was	All/most/some/none
Breakfast		
Snack		
Lunch		
Dessert		
Snack		
Dinner		
Dessert		

Please sign the medicine book ☐ Please provide some more:

Please sign the accident book ☐ _____

Today I slept...

Fell Asleep	Woke Up

Today my nappies were...

Time	Wet	Soiled	Dry	Checked

I had the following milk today...

Time	fl oz	Time	fl oz

Today I...

Went on the potty ☐   Went on the toilet ☐   I tried! ☐

Additional Notes...

Date ⬭

Today I have been...

Happy ☐	Chatty ☐	Quiet ☐	Sad ☐	Funny ☐	Tired ☐
Grumpy ☐	Noisy ☐	Friendly ☐	Ill ☐	Rebellious ☐	Energetic ☐

The activities I did today were...

Today I learnt about...

Today I have eaten...

Meal	What it was	All/most/some/none
Breakfast		
Snack		
Lunch		
Dessert		
Snack		
Dinner		
Dessert		

Please sign the medicine book ☐   Please provide some more:

Please sign the accident book ☐   _____

Today I slept...

Fell Asleep	Woke Up

Today my nappies were...

Time	Wet	Soiled	Dry	Checked

I had the following milk today...

Time	fl oz	Time	fl oz

Today I...

 Went on the potty ☐ Went on the toilet ☐ I tried! ☐

Additional Notes...

Date (_____)

Today I have been...

| Happy ☐ | Chatty ☐ | Quiet ☐ | Sad ☐ | Funny ☐ | Tired ☐ |

| Grumpy ☐ | Noisy ☐ | Friendly ☐ | Ill ☐ | Rebellious ☐ | Energetic ☐ |

The activities I did today were...

Today I learnt about...

Today I have eaten...

Meal	What it was	All/most/some/none
Breakfast		
Snack		
Lunch		
Dessert		
Snack		
Dinner		
Dessert		

Please sign the medicine book ☐   Please provide some more:

Please sign the accident book ☐   _____

Today I slept...

Fell Asleep	Woke Up

Today my nappies were...

Time	Wet	Soiled	Dry	Checked

I had the following milk today...

Time	fl oz	Time	fl oz

Today I...

Went on the potty ☐   Went on the toilet ☐   I tried! ☐

Additional Notes...

Date ( )

Today I have been...

Happy ☐   Chatty ☐   Quiet ☐   Sad ☐   Funny ☐   Tired ☐

Grumpy ☐   Noisy ☐   Friendly ☐   Ill ☐   Rebellious ☐   Energetic ☐

The activities I did today were...

Today I learnt about...

Today I have eaten...

Meal	What it was	All/most/some/none
Breakfast		
Snack		
Lunch		
Dessert		
Snack		
Dinner		
Dessert		

Please sign the medicine book ☐   Please provide some more:

Please sign the accident book ☐   _____

Today I slept...

Fell Asleep	Woke Up

Today my nappies were...

Time	Wet	Soiled	Dry	Checked

I had the following milk today...

Time	fl oz	Time	fl oz

Today I...

Went on the potty ☐   Went on the toilet ☐   I tried! ☐

Additional Notes...

Date (   )

Today I have been...

Happy ☐	Chatty ☐	Quiet ☐	Sad ☐	Funny ☐	Tired ☐

Grumpy ☐	Noisy ☐	Friendly ☐	Ill ☐	Rebellious ☐	Energetic ☐

The activities I did today were...

Today I learnt about...

Today I have eaten...

Meal	What it was	All/most/some/none
Breakfast		
Snack		
Lunch		
Dessert		
Snack		
Dinner		
Dessert		

Please sign the medicine book ☐   Please provide some more:

Please sign the accident book ☐   _____

Today I slept...

Fell Asleep	Woke Up

Today my nappies were...

Time	Wet	Soiled	Dry	Checked

I had the following milk today...

Time	fl oz	Time	fl oz

Today I...

Went on the potty ☐   Went on the toilet ☐   I tried! ☐

Additional Notes...

Observations

This weekend I...

Weekly Planning

	Trips	Activities	Notes
Monday			
Tuesday			
Wednesday			
Thursday			
Friday			

Parent's Notes

Monday

Tuesday

Wednesday

Thursday

Friday

Date ( )

Today I have been...

Happy ☐ Chatty ☐ Quiet ☐ Sad ☐ Funny ☐ Tired ☐

Grumpy ☐ Noisy ☐ Friendly ☐ Ill ☐ Rebellious ☐ Energetic ☐

The activities I did today were...

Today I learnt about...

Today I have eaten...

Meal	What it was	All/most/some/none
Breakfast		
Snack		
Lunch		
Dessert		
Snack		
Dinner		
Dessert		

Please sign the medicine book ☐ Please provide some more:

Please sign the accident book ☐ _____

Today I slept...

Fell Asleep	Woke Up

Today my nappies were...

Time	Wet	Soiled	Dry	Checked

I had the following milk today...

Time	fl oz	Time	fl oz

Today I...

Went on the potty ☐   Went on the toilet ☐   I tried! ☐

Additional Notes...

Date ( )

Today I have been...

Happy ☐   Chatty ☐   Quiet ☐   Sad ☐   Funny ☐   Tired ☐

Grumpy ☐   Noisy ☐   Friendly ☐   Ill ☐   Rebellious ☐   Energetic ☐

The activities I did today were...

Today I learnt about...

Today I have eaten...

Meal	What it was	All/most/some/none
Breakfast		
Snack		
Lunch		
Dessert		
Snack		
Dinner		
Dessert		

Please sign the medicine book ☐   Please provide some more:

Please sign the accident book ☐   _____

Today I slept...

Fell Asleep	Woke Up

Today my nappies were...

Time	Wet	Soiled	Dry	Checked

I had the following milk today...

Time	fl oz	Time	fl oz

Today I...

Went on the potty ☐   Went on the toilet ☐   I tried! ☐

Additional Notes...

Date ⌈_____⌉

Today I have been...

Happy ☐　Chatty ☐　Quiet ☐　Sad ☐　Funny ☐　Tired ☐

Grumpy ☐　Noisy ☐　Friendly ☐　Ill ☐　Rebellious ☐　Energetic ☐

The activities I did today were...

⌈_____⌉

Today I learnt about...

⌈_____⌉

Today I have eaten...

Meal	What it was	All/most/some/none
Breakfast		
Snack		
Lunch		
Dessert		
Snack		
Dinner		
Dessert		

Please sign the medicine book ☐　Please provide some more:

Please sign the accident book ☐　_____

Today I slept...

Fell Asleep	Woke Up

Today my nappies were...

Time	Wet	Soiled	Dry	Checked

I had the following milk today...

Time	fl oz	Time	fl oz

Today I...

Went on the potty ☐   Went on the toilet ☐   I tried! ☐

Additional Notes...

Date ⬭

Today I have been...

Happy ☐   Chatty ☐   Quiet ☐   Sad ☐   Funny ☐   Tired ☐

Grumpy ☐   Noisy ☐   Friendly ☐   Ill ☐   Rebellious ☐   Energetic ☐

The activities I did today were...

Today I learnt about...

Today I have eaten...

Meal	What it was	All/most/some/none
Breakfast		
Snack		
Lunch		
Dessert		
Snack		
Dinner		
Dessert		

Please sign the medicine book ☐   Please provide some more:

Please sign the accident book ☐   _____

Today I slept...

Fell Asleep	Woke Up

Today my nappies were...

Time	Wet	Soiled	Dry	Checked

I had the following milk today...

Time	fl oz	Time	fl oz

Today I...

Went on the potty ☐   Went on the toilet ☐   I tried! ☐

Additional Notes...

Date

Today I have been...

Happy ☐ Chatty ☐ Quiet ☐ Sad ☐ Funny ☐ Tired ☐

Grumpy ☐ Noisy ☐ Friendly ☐ Ill ☐ Rebellious ☐ Energetic ☐

The activities I did today were...

Today I learnt about...

Today I have eaten...

Meal	What it was	All/most/some/none
Breakfast		
Snack		
Lunch		
Dessert		
Snack		
Dinner		
Dessert		

Please sign the medicine book ☐   Please provide some more:

Please sign the accident book ☐   _____

Today I slept...

Fell Asleep	Woke Up

Today my nappies were...

Time	Wet	Soiled	Dry	Checked

I had the following milk today...

Time	fl oz	Time	fl oz

Today I...

Went on the potty ☐   Went on the toilet ☐   I tried! ☐

Additional Notes...

Observations

This weekend I...

Weekly Planning

	Trips	Activities	Notes
Monday			
Tuesday			
Wednesday			
Thursday			
Friday			

Parent's Notes

Monday
Tuesday
Wednesday
Thursday
Friday

Date [   ]

Today I have been...

| Happy ☐ | Chatty ☐ | Quiet ☐ | Sad ☐ | Funny ☐ | Tired ☐ |
| Grumpy ☐ | Noisy ☐ | Friendly ☐ | Ill ☐ | Rebellious ☐ | Energetic ☐ |

The activities I did today were...

[   ]

Today I learnt about...

[   ]

Today I have eaten...

Meal	What it was	All/most/some/none
Breakfast		
Snack		
Lunch		
Dessert		
Snack		
Dinner		
Dessert		

Please sign the medicine book ☐   Please provide some more:

Please sign the accident book ☐   _____

Today I slept...

Fell Asleep	Woke Up

Today my nappies were...

Time	Wet	Soiled	Dry	Checked

I had the following milk today...

Time	fl oz	Time	fl oz

Today I...

Went on the potty ☐   Went on the toilet ☐   I tried! ☐

Additional Notes...

Date (_____)

Today I have been...

Happy ☐	Chatty ☐	Quiet ☐	Sad ☐	Funny ☐	Tired ☐
Grumpy ☐	Noisy ☐	Friendly ☐	Ill ☐	Rebellious ☐	Energetic ☐

The activities I did today were...

Today I learnt about...

Today I have eaten...

Meal	What it was	All/most/some/none
Breakfast		
Snack		
Lunch		
Dessert		
Snack		
Dinner		
Dessert		

Please sign the medicine book ☐   Please provide some more:

Please sign the accident book ☐   _____

Today I slept...

Fell Asleep	Woke Up

Today my nappies were...

Time	Wet	Soiled	Dry	Checked

I had the following milk today...

Time	fl oz	Time	fl oz

Today I...

Went on the potty ☐   Went on the toilet ☐   I tried! ☐

Additional Notes...

Date ⬭

Today I have been...

| Happy ☐ | Chatty ☐ | Quiet ☐ | Sad ☐ | Funny ☐ | Tired ☐ |

| Grumpy ☐ | Noisy ☐ | Friendly ☐ | Ill ☐ | Rebellious ☐ | Energetic ☐ |

The activities I did today were...

Today I learnt about...

Today I have eaten...

Meal	What it was	All/most/some/none
Breakfast		
Snack		
Lunch		
Dessert		
Snack		
Dinner		
Dessert		

Please sign the medicine book ☐   Please provide some more:

Please sign the accident book ☐   _____

Today I slept...

Fell Asleep	Woke Up

Today my nappies were...

Time	Wet	Soiled	Dry	Checked

I had the following milk today...

Time	fl oz	Time	fl oz

Today I...

Went on the potty ☐ Went on the toilet ☐ I tried! ☐

Additional Notes...

Date ⬭

Today I have been...

Happy ☐	Chatty ☐	Quiet ☐	Sad ☐	Funny ☐	Tired ☐
Grumpy ☐	Noisy ☐	Friendly ☐	Ill ☐	Rebellious ☐	Energetic ☐

The activities I did today were...

Today I learnt about...

Today I have eaten...

Meal	What it was	All/most/some/none
Breakfast		
Snack		
Lunch		
Dessert		
Snack		
Dinner		
Dessert		

Please sign the medicine book ☐   Please provide some more:

Please sign the accident book ☐   _____

Today I slept...

Fell Asleep	Woke Up

Today my nappies were...

Time	Wet	Soiled	Dry	Checked

I had the following milk today...

Time	fl oz	Time	fl oz

Today I...

Went on the potty ☐   Went on the toilet ☐   I tried! ☐

Additional Notes...

Date ( )

Today I have been...

Happy ☐ Chatty ☐ Quiet ☐ Sad ☐ Funny ☐ Tired ☐

Grumpy ☐ Noisy ☐ Friendly ☐ Ill ☐ Rebellious ☐ Energetic ☐

The activities I did today were...

Today I learnt about...

Today I have eaten...

Meal	What it was	All/most/some/none
Breakfast		
Snack		
Lunch		
Dessert		
Snack		
Dinner		
Dessert		

Please sign the medicine book ☐   Please provide some more:

Please sign the accident book ☐   _____

Today I slept...

Fell Asleep	Woke Up

Today my nappies were...

Time	Wet	Soiled	Dry	Checked

I had the following milk today...

Time	fl oz	Time	fl oz

Today I...

 Went on the potty ☐ Went on the toilet ☐ I tried! ☐

Additional Notes...

Observations

This weekend I...

Weekly Planning

	Trips	Activities	Notes
Monday			
Tuesday			
Wednesday			
Thursday			
Friday			

Parent's Notes

Monday

Tuesday

Wednesday

Thursday

Friday

Date _____

Today I have been...

Happy ☐	Chatty ☐	Quiet ☐	Sad ☐	Funny ☐	Tired ☐
Grumpy ☐	Noisy ☐	Friendly ☐	Ill ☐	Rebellious ☐	Energetic ☐

The activities I did today were...

_____

Today I learnt about...

_____

Today I have eaten...

Meal	What it was	All/most/some/none
Breakfast		
Snack		
Lunch		
Dessert		
Snack		
Dinner		
Dessert		

Please sign the medicine book ☐   Please provide some more:

Please sign the accident book ☐   _____

Today I slept...

Fell Asleep	Woke Up

Today my nappies were...

Time	Wet	Soiled	Dry	Checked

I had the following milk today...

Time	fl oz	Time	fl oz

Today I...

Went on the potty ☐   Went on the toilet ☐   I tried! ☐

Additional Notes...

Date ( )

Today I have been...

Happy ☐	Chatty ☐	Quiet ☐	Sad ☐	Funny ☐	Tired ☐
Grumpy ☐	Noisy ☐	Friendly ☐	Ill ☐	Rebellious ☐	Energetic ☐

The activities I did today were...

Today I learnt about...

Today I have eaten...

Meal	What it was	All/most/some/none
Breakfast		
Snack		
Lunch		
Dessert		
Snack		
Dinner		
Dessert		

Please sign the medicine book ☐   Please provide some more:

Please sign the accident book ☐   _____

Today I slept...

Fell Asleep	Woke Up

Today my nappies were...

Time	Wet	Soiled	Dry	Checked

I had the following milk today...

Time	fl oz	Time	fl oz

Today I...

Went on the potty ☐   Went on the toilet ☐   I tried! ☐

Additional Notes...

Date (_____)

Today I have been...

Happy ☐	Chatty ☐	Quiet ☐	Sad ☐	Funny ☐	Tired ☐
Grumpy ☐	Noisy ☐	Friendly ☐	Ill ☐	Rebellious ☐	Energetic ☐

The activities I did today were...

Today I learnt about...

Today I have eaten...

Meal	What it was	All/most/some/none
Breakfast		
Snack		
Lunch		
Dessert		
Snack		
Dinner		
Dessert		

Please sign the medicine book ☐   Please provide some more:

Please sign the accident book ☐   _____

Today I slept...

Fell Asleep	Woke Up

Today my nappies were...

Time	Wet	Soiled	Dry	Checked

I had the following milk today...

Time	fl oz	Time	fl oz

Today I...

Went on the potty ☐ Went on the toilet ☐ I tried! ☐

Additional Notes...

Date (_____)

Today I have been...

Happy ☐	Chatty ☐	Quiet ☐	Sad ☐	Funny ☐	Tired ☐
Grumpy ☐	Noisy ☐	Friendly ☐	Ill ☐	Rebellious ☐	Energetic ☐

The activities I did today were...

Today I learnt about...

Today I have eaten...

Meal	What it was	All/most/some/none
Breakfast		
Snack		
Lunch		
Dessert		
Snack		
Dinner		
Dessert		

Please sign the medicine book ☐   Please provide some more:

Please sign the accident book ☐   _____

Today I slept...

Fell Asleep	Woke Up

Today my nappies were...

Time	Wet	Soiled	Dry	Checked

I had the following milk today...

Time	fl oz	Time	fl oz

Today I...

Went on the potty ☐   Went on the toilet ☐   I tried! ☐

Additional Notes...

Date

Today I have been...

Happy ☐ Chatty ☐ Quiet ☐ Sad ☐ Funny ☐ Tired ☐

Grumpy ☐ Noisy ☐ Friendly ☐ Ill ☐ Rebellious ☐ Energetic ☐

The activities I did today were...

Today I learnt about...

Today I have eaten...

Meal	What it was	All/most/some/none
Breakfast		
Snack		
Lunch		
Dessert		
Snack		
Dinner		
Dessert		

Please sign the medicine book ☐   Please provide some more:

Please sign the accident book ☐   _____

Today I slept...

Fell Asleep	Woke Up

Today my nappies were...

Time	Wet	Soiled	Dry	Checked

I had the following milk today...

Time	fl oz	Time	fl oz

Today I...

Went on the potty ☐   Went on the toilet ☐   I tried! ☐

Additional Notes...

Observations

This weekend I...

Weekly Planning

	Trips	Activities	Notes
Monday			
Tuesday			
Wednesday			
Thursday			
Friday			

Parent's Notes

Monday

Tuesday

Wednesday

Thursday

Friday

Date

Today I have been...

Happy ☐   Chatty ☐   Quiet ☐   Sad ☐   Funny ☐   Tired ☐

Grumpy ☐   Noisy ☐   Friendly ☐   Ill ☐   Rebellious ☐   Energetic ☐

The activities I did today were...

Today I learnt about...

Today I have eaten...

Meal	What it was	All/most/some/none
Breakfast		
Snack		
Lunch		
Dessert		
Snack		
Dinner		
Dessert		

Please sign the medicine book ☐   Please provide some more:

Please sign the accident book ☐   _____

Today I slept...

Fell Asleep	Woke Up

Today my nappies were...

Time	Wet	Soiled	Dry	Checked

I had the following milk today...

Time	fl oz	Time	fl oz

Today I...

Went on the potty ☐   Went on the toilet ☐   I tried! ☐

Additional Notes...

Date ( )

Today I have been...

Happy ☐	Chatty ☐	Quiet ☐	Sad ☐	Funny ☐	Tired ☐
Grumpy ☐	Noisy ☐	Friendly ☐	Ill ☐	Rebellious ☐	Energetic ☐

The activities I did today were...

Today I learnt about...

Today I have eaten...

Meal	What it was	All/most/some/none
Breakfast		
Snack		
Lunch		
Dessert		
Snack		
Dinner		
Dessert		

Please sign the medicine book ☐   Please provide some more:

Please sign the accident book ☐   _____

Today I slept...

Fell Asleep	Woke Up

Today my nappies were...

Time	Wet	Soiled	Dry	Checked

I had the following milk today...

Time	fl oz	Time	fl oz

Today I...

Went on the potty ☐ Went on the toilet ☐ I tried! ☐

Additional Notes...

Date ⬭

Today I have been...

Happy ☐	Chatty ☐	Quiet ☐	Sad ☐	Funny ☐	Tired ☐
Grumpy ☐	Noisy ☐	Friendly ☐	Ill ☐	Rebellious ☐	Energetic ☐

The activities I did today were...

Today I learnt about...

Today I have eaten...

Meal	What it was	All/most/some/none
Breakfast		
Snack		
Lunch		
Dessert		
Snack		
Dinner		
Dessert		

Please sign the medicine book ☐   Please provide some more:

Please sign the accident book ☐   _____

Today I slept...

Fell Asleep	Woke Up

Today my nappies were...

Time	Wet	Soiled	Dry	Checked

I had the following milk today...

Time	fl oz	Time	fl oz

Today I...

Went on the potty ☐   Went on the toilet ☐   I tried! ☐

Additional Notes...

Date

Today I have been...

Happy ☐ Chatty ☐ Quiet ☐ Sad ☐ Funny ☐ Tired ☐

Grumpy ☐ Noisy ☐ Friendly ☐ Ill ☐ Rebellious ☐ Energetic ☐

The activities I did today were...

Today I learnt about...

Today I have eaten...

Meal	What it was	All/most/some/none
Breakfast		
Snack		
Lunch		
Dessert		
Snack		
Dinner		
Dessert		

Please sign the medicine book ☐   Please provide some more:

Please sign the accident book ☐   _____

Today I slept...

Fell Asleep	Woke Up

Today my nappies were...

Time	Wet	Soiled	Dry	Checked

I had the following milk today...

Time	fl oz	Time	fl oz

Today I...

Went on the potty ☐   Went on the toilet ☐   I tried! ☐

Additional Notes...

Date (_____)

Today I have been...

Happy ☐	Chatty ☐	Quiet ☐	Sad ☐	Funny ☐	Tired ☐
Grumpy ☐	Noisy ☐	Friendly ☐	Ill ☐	Rebellious ☐	Energetic ☐

The activities I did today were...

Today I learnt about...

Today I have eaten...

Meal	What it was	All/most/some/none
Breakfast		
Snack		
Lunch		
Dessert		
Snack		
Dinner		
Dessert		

Please sign the medicine book ☐   Please provide some more:

Please sign the accident book ☐   _____

Today I slept...

Fell Asleep	Woke Up

Today my nappies were...

Time	Wet	Soiled	Dry	Checked

I had the following milk today...

Time	fl oz	Time	fl oz

Today I...

Went on the potty ☐   Went on the toilet ☐   I tried! ☐

Additional Notes...

Observations

The Essential Childminder Magazine

Written for childminders by childminders
www.essentialchildminder.co.uk

Packed full of planning ideas, early years news and information, competitions and much, much more.

Perfect for parents; providing ideas to keep all your children entertained and to learn more about the needs and development of your children.

Inspiring for all early years practitioners to help you think outside the box and to assist you in your settings.